Autonomous Vehicles and the Future of Auto Insurance

KARLYN D. STANLEY, MICHELLE GRISÉ, JAMES M. ANDERSON

T0306489

RAND SOCIAL AND ECONOMIC WELL BEING

For more information on this publication, visit www.rand.org/t/RRA878-1

Library of Congress Cataloging-in-Publication Data is available for this publication.
ISBN: 978-1-9774-0635-4

Published by the RAND Corporation, Santa Monica, Calif.
© Copyright 2020 RAND Corporation
RAND® is a registered trademark.

Cover: kadmy/Getty Images/iStockphoto (crashed car); Bill Oxford/Getty Images/iStockphoto (insurance form).

Support RAND
Make a tax-deductible charitable contribution at
www.rand.org/giving/contribute

www.rand.org

Preface

Researchers at the RAND Institute for Civil Justice (ICJ) conducted the study reported here to investigate the potential impact that the introduction of autonomous vehicles could have on the U.S. automobile insurance system. In addition to its support from the pooled contributions of the ICJ, this research was supported by the American Insurance Association (now the American Property Casualty Insurance Association) and The Travelers Companies.

The RAND Institute for Civil Justice

The ICJ is dedicated to improving the civil justice system by supplying policymakers and the public with rigorous and nonpartisan research. Its studies identify trends in litigation and inform policy choices concerning liability, compensation, regulation, risk management, and insurance. The institute builds on a long tradition of RAND Corporation research characterized by an interdisciplinary, empirical approach to public policy issues and rigorous standards of quality, objectivity, and independence. ICJ research is supported by pooled grants from a range of sources, including corporations, trade and professional associations, individuals, government agencies, and private foundations. All its reports are subject to peer review and disseminated widely to policymakers, practitioners in law and business, other researchers, and the public. The ICJ is part of the Justice Policy Program within the RAND Social and Economic Well-Being Division. The program focuses on such topics as access to justice, policing, corrections, drug policy, and court system reform, as well as other policy concerns pertaining to public safety and criminal and civil justice. For more information, email justicepolicy@rand.org.

Contents

Figures and Tables

Figures

Tables

Summary

What will increasing adoption of autonomous vehicles (AVs) mean for auto insurance?

To answer this question, we first define some key terms. The National Highway Traffic Safety Administration (NHTSA) has adopted a system created by the Society of Automotive Engineers (SAE) to describe the levels of vehicle automation. The scale goes from 0 (no automation) to 5 (full automation) (NHTSA, undated a). Vehicles operating at Level 0, 1, 2, or 3 we call *automated*. In this report, we discuss vehicles we call *autonomous*—those that operate at Level 4 or 5:

- At **Level 4**, or **high automation**, "[a]n automated driving system (ADS) on the vehicle can itself perform all driving tasks and monitor the driving environment— essentially, do all the driving—in *certain* circumstances. The human need not pay attention in those circumstances" (NHTSA, undated a; emphasis ours).
- At **Level 5**, or **full automation**, "[a]n automated driving system (ADS) on the vehicle can do all the driving in *all* circumstances. The human occupants are just passengers and need never be involved in driving" (NHTSA, undated a; emphasis ours).

Although the rate of adoption of transportation automation remains uncertain, vehicles have become increasingly automated. Currently, many new car models incorporate **driver assistance technologies**, described by NHTSA (NHTSA, undated b) as including

- forward collision warnings
- automatic emergency braking
- pedestrian automatic emergency braking (detects, warns the driver about, and, if necessary, automatically brakes for a pedestrian crossing in front of the vehicle)
- adaptive lighting
- adaptive cruise control
- lane departure warnings
- rearview video systems
- rear cross-traffic alerts.

Increasingly, forms of driver assistance that combine lane keeping with adaptive cruise control are being introduced (NHTSA, undated b). Many of these new systems, particularly automatic emergency braking, represent an important step toward improving the safety of new cars. However, the gradual development and deployment of these new systems represents a challenge for regulators and industry stakeholders. The roads of the near future will be home to both AVs, including vehicles with significant variability in the extent of their automated features, and vehicles that lack automation (Level 0, at which the "driver performs all driving tasks" [NHTSA, undated a]). As a result, the impact that AVs will have on the automobile insurance industry is unclear.[1]

Automobile insurance is an important consideration in the deployment of vehicles that incorporate technologies that will permit autonomous operation at most times. This is true both from the standpoint of compliance with existing state regulations and from the perspective of consumer confidence in these new technologies. The potential benefits of AV technologies are significant. Most importantly, AVs have the potential to save lives and prevent injuries. Annually, conventional car crashes cause approximately 4.5 million injuries and 36,560 fatalities in the United States (NHTSA, undated b; National Safety Council, undated). For the National Motor Vehicle Crash Causation Survey, researchers studied crashes from a two-year period. They determined that "[t]he critical reason, which is the last event in the crash causal chain, was assigned to the driver in 94 percent (±2.2%) of the crashes" (NHTSA, 2015, p. 1). In 2016, NHTSA stated that it was working to "address the human choices that are linked to 94 percent of serious crashes" (NHTSA, 2017). It also stated that it

> continues to promote vehicle technologies that hold the potential to reduce the number of crashes and save thousands of lives every year, and may eventually help reduce or eliminate human error and the mistakes that drivers make behind the wheel. (NHTSA, 2017)

In addition, vehicles that incorporate technologies that permit autonomous operation at all or most times will provide numerous social benefits, including increasing the mobility of tens of millions of Americans who cannot drive because of, for example, disability or age (Halsey, 2017). Technologies for automating vehicles may also reduce traffic congestion and facilitate more-efficient land use and urban planning (Anderson, Kalra, Stanley, Sorensen, et al., 2016). However, if the U.S. auto fleet is saturated with Level 4 and 5 vehicles,[2] there could be some improvements in traffic flow management (e.g., consistent speeds and following distances between vehicles) but diminished effi-

---

[1] For earlier work on the liability implications of AVs, see Anderson, Kalra, Stanley, Sorensen, et al., 2016; Kalra, Anderson, and Wachs, 2009; Logue, 2019; and Crane, Logue, and Pilz, 2017.

[2] The levels are part of an Automated Vehicle Safety Consortium–developed system for categorizing vehicles with varying levels of automation. The six levels start at 0 (no automation) and proceed to 5 (full automation, in which the "vehicle is capable of performing all driving functions under all conditions. The driver may have the

ciencies due to increased traffic density and volume from theorized benefits, such as the increase in mobility for youth, elderly, and disabled populations. Traffic patterns and congestion could get worse during the long-tailed transition with a mixed fleet of conventional and autonomous vehicles (Anderson, Kalra, Stanley, Sorensen, et al., 2016). At the same time, the introduction of AVs is likely to create uncertainty in regulation and insurance.[3] The challenge for policymakers will be maximizing the benefits associated with AVs while reducing the uncertainty occasioned by their introduction.

From a theoretical perspective, there are several reasons to think that automation will lead to a shift in liability from the individual driver (and the driver's insurer) to the manufacturer. The primary historical justifications of tort law offer some rationales for such a shift. Existing products liability law doctrines, including product defect and failure to warn, could readily apply to crashes involving automated and autonomous vehicles. Indeed, products liability's doctrinal focus on design defects and failure to warn is arguably more relevant to crashes involving AVs than an analysis that focuses on driver performance would be. To be clear, this is a descriptive prediction of how courts and legal analysts are likely to apply the predominant justifications of tort law to this new technology and not a normative argument either in favor of or against doing so. For fleet operators, it is also likely that there will be a shift toward manufacturer liability, although that question is more complex.[4]

There are numerous practical reasons, however, to think that this shift toward manufacturer liability will be more gradual. The sheer volume of auto crashes requires a vast infrastructure of specialists who resolve and adjudicate these claims and make the needed repairs. Insurers have considerable specialized expertise in this role. It is unlikely that manufacturers will replicate this infrastructure overnight or that individuals will soon view products liability against manufacturers as the obvious institution to resolve a minor crash.

It seems likely that manufacturers will increasingly compete with traditional auto insurers and offer insurance packaged with their vehicles. Tesla, for example, has announced that it will do so (Moorcraft, 2019). To the extent that the primary determinants of crashes are vehicle characteristics rather than driver characteristics, manufacturers may, in fact, be in the best position to collect data and underwrite the risks as efficiently as possible. Similarly, if automation dramatically reduces claim frequency, it may reduce the scale of infrastructure necessary. Insurance bundled with the price of the vehicle may be an attractive concept for some consumers. But it is also possible that

---

option to control the vehicle" (NHTSA, undated a). The consortium is a project of SAE International and the SAE Industry Technologies Consortia, so the levels are often called SAE levels.

[3] For further discussion of the uncertainty created by the introduction of AVs from a cybersecurity perspective, see Winkelman et al., 2019a; Winkelman et al., 2019b; and Dreyer et al., 2018.

[4] Chapter Two of the report, which covers tort law, was used to develop the evaluation criteria for future AV insurance models discussed in Chapter Three.

manufacturers will decide that underwriting, regulatory compliance, and handling of claims are outside their core competencies and either outsource those functions or leave the provision of insurance products to insurers.

Operators of fleets of AVs may also serve an important role in serving as transportation providers. They may self-insure and have the size and expertise to subrogate claims against manufacturers when appropriate. It is possible that such fleets will decrease the rate of private car ownership and the demand for private auto insurance.[5]

Policymakers do not need to fundamentally change automobile insurance law to see technology to automate vehicles advance. Currently, insurance is governed by states, and each state sets its own particular requirements and requires rate approval. This makes some sense in the U.S. federal system because tort law is primarily a function of the state. This also permits a state-by-state determination of financial solvency and rates.[6]

To investigate the potential impact that the introduction of AVs could have on the U.S. automobile insurance industry, we interviewed a broad variety of stakeholders, including representatives from automobile insurance companies, original equipment manufacturers (OEMs), state and federal governments, consumer advocacy groups, ride-sharing companies, AV and trucking start-ups, industry associations, and academia. We also interviewed plaintiff's lawyers and defense lawyers who practice in this field. Finally, we interviewed experts and regulators in Japan, Australia, Canada, and the United Kingdom. This report captures the perspectives of 43 subject-matter experts from 35 organizations.

We discussed five potential insurance frameworks with stakeholders:

- national no-fault insurance, analogous to the vaccine or nuclear statutory insurance program (in this report, we refer to this as *national no-fault*)
- state no-fault insurance, an option available in those states that provide for it in state law (in this report, we refer to this as *state no-fault*)
- self-insurance by manufacturers
- fleet insurance policies
- adaptation of the existing automobile insurance framework.

---

[5] One stakeholder noted, "They may be obligated to self-insure up to higher-than-anticipated retentions, based on the fact that there is no data on which insurers can appropriately price liability policies."

[6] A state-by-state system does pose a significant burden to new entrants who might want to offer new insurance products. If policymakers wanted to increase competition and potentially permit new entrants, they could consider (1) a federal insurance charter so that an insurer would have only to clear one set of federal regulatory barriers to offer insurance in the country or (2) liberalizing and standardizing state-by-state requirements.

There may also be future tension over data availability. Currently, the most-relevant information in determining risk is past human driving behavior that insurers and regulators use during the rate and solvency approval process. As automation supplants human driving, these data become less relevant, and data on the operation of the automation become more relevant. These data, however, are possessed by the manufacturer, which is not party to the rate and solvency regulatory process.

We addressed nine distinct research questions. Our findings are briefly outlined in the rest of this summary.

Will the introduction of AVs that have Level 4 or 5 capabilities require significant changes to the existing U.S. automobile insurance system, or is the current insurance model flexible enough to handle vehicles that incorporate technologies that permit autonomous operation at most or all times? A majority of U.S. stakeholders, representing both manufacturers and the insurance industry, expressed optimism that the existing insurance framework would be able to adapt to the deployment of AVs. Less than half of the experts who thought the current auto insurance framework would persist suggested that the existing automobile insurance system in the United States would not be able to adapt to AVs. Several of these experts indicated that, when a vehicle is operating autonomously, liability will have to shift away from the driver and the cost of insurance will be bundled with the vehicle.

However, a large majority of stakeholders, including those who anticipated changes in the insurance industry, thought that the status quo would persist for the foreseeable future. Those who foresaw changes in the industry were split as to whether those changes would occur at Level 3 or 4, with the majority asserting that changes would occur at Level 4.

What are the benefits and drawbacks of potential future models for automobile insurance? The criteria used to define benefits and drawbacks for potential future models for auto insurance (national no-fault, state no-fault, self-insurance by manufacturers, and fleet insurance policies) were (1) whether legislative action would be required, (2) potential incentive or disincentive for manufacturer product safety improvements, (3) fraud concerns, (4) ease of the claims process, and (5) application to all levels of automation. The report provides a discussion of national no-fault, state no-fault, manufacturer self-insurance, and fleet insurance, as well as a detailed analysis of expert views on the benefits and drawbacks of these potential future auto insurance models.

The experts discussed the potential benefits of national no-fault auto insurance and state no-fault insurance as possible future models for auto insurance. Although some experts thought that, in a future in which most vehicles on the road have Level 4 capabilities, a no-fault framework might be beneficial and easy, the majority of experts rejected the idea of adopting the current state no-fault system in the future. This was primarily because of the experts' expressed concern that a national no-fault system modeled on current state no-fault programs would fail to provide adequate incentive for manufacturers to improve their AVs.

A large majority of the experts we interviewed dismissed the idea of national no-fault as impractical, because it would require congressional legislation and because a government-run claims system was perceived to be unwieldy and unlikely to swiftly provide compensation for the injured.

Several experts were proponents of self-insurance by manufacturers. These experts thought that OEMs might purchase insurance companies and have them handle the insurance for their AVs. According to several experts, this would allow OEMs to bundle insurance with the sale of AVs, which might provide the benefit of indicating to consumers that the OEMs considered their vehicles to be safe. One expert thought that bundling insurance with the price of an AV might serve as a competitive advantage. Some experts viewed self-insurance by manufacturers skeptically unless an experienced insurance company was involved. The skeptical experts pointed out that auto insurance was not a core competency of OEMs; it requires licensing in 50 states and a smoothly functioning claims process. Many of the stakeholders we interviewed, however, did not express an opinion about self-insurance by manufacturers.

A significant majority of the experts acknowledged fleet insurance as being a likely future model for insuring AVs. Experts commented that it would have the benefit of being based on existing models for fleet insurance, with a well-established claims process to compensate the injured.

What is the likelihood that vehicles that incorporate technologies that permit autonomous operation at most or all times will be insured in fleets rather than by individual policy holders? A majority of the stakeholders we interviewed expected that AVs would initially be deployed in fleets. Insurance companies, we were told, will handle AV fleets "the way they always have." That is, the owners of fleets will choose to self-insure or to purchase insurance under corporate general liability policies. Fleet insurance was acknowledged by a significant majority of the experts as being a likely future model for insuring AVs. Experts commented that it would have the benefit of being based on existing models for fleet insurance, with a well-established claims process to compensate the injured. However, the future dominance of the fleet insurance model was not seen as inevitable. Although most stakeholders believed that the fleet model was likely to become dominant, one manufacturer cautioned that it was still too soon to develop "any concrete business model" for the deployment of AVs in fleets. In addition, stakeholders noted that it is important to think about the broader societal implications of relying on fleets for daily transportation needs.

Is the subrogation process likely to change in future models for automobile insurance? Most stakeholders indicated that the deployment of AVs would not affect subrogation. Subrogation is a "big part of what [insurers] do" today, and insurers told us that they would continue to handle the subrogation process in the same way. Although the deployment of AVs may create a more complex ecosystem of suppliers and, in some cases, make it more difficult to determine which supplier was at fault, insurers anticipated continuing to "handle this like [they] handle suppliers today.".

In the future, how might accidents between AVs and conventional vehicles and between AVs and pedestrians be handled? A majority of stakeholders indicated that, for accidents involving AVs and conventional cars, the claims process would not change significantly. In contrast to the claims process, however, one expert indicated that, for an accident involving severe injuries, the injured party might consider suing the AV manufacturer if the losses exceeded the policy limit of the AV driver or owner. Many stakeholders indicated that accidents between AVs and pedestrians would be handled the same way as those between conventional cars and pedestrians.

Will minor accidents and "fender benders" become significantly more expensive because of the cost of repairing the sensors in AVs, or is this concern overblown? The experts we interviewed were generally in agreement that the sensors that are part of AV technologies would increase the cost of accidents involving AVs, at least initially. Experts differed, however, in their assessments of the extent of this impact. Other experts minimized the potential impact of the cost of sensors and sensor repair, stating that AVs at Levels 4 and 5 are going to be involved in fewer collisions because of the sensor technology embedded within them and that, therefore, the overall cost to the industry probably will be about equal to what it is today.

How might changes to accommodate AV technologies in the insurance models of other countries inform changes to U.S. automobile insurance? We investigated how four countries—the United Kingdom, Australia, Canada, and Japan—were adapting their insurance frameworks to accommodate AVs. We were especially interested in these countries because their insurance frameworks are centered on a commitment to adequately and efficiently compensating the injured. We compared the frameworks of these four countries according to ten criteria. All of the countries have a focus on swift and easy compensation for victims of an accident. For this reason, reliance on products liability litigation was not the most favored approach to victim compensation.[7] All of the countries we investigated followed an adaptive approach to incorporating AVs into auto insurance schemes. The experts we consulted indicated that the current framework for auto insurance would be flexible enough to accommodate AVs up to Level 3 but that, once most vehicles could operate at Level 4 or 5, the auto insurance framework might need to change. Similarly, it appeared that although countries were preparing to deal with the new challenges that might be posed by AVs, policymakers intended to assess developments with the technology before undertaking any major overhaul of the existing auto insurance framework. As one Australian expert noted, Australian regulators recognize that what they develop needs to be proportional and scalable over time. Other countries, such as the UK and Japan, are focused on having insurance coverage for all drivers. Policymakers in several countries, such as the UK, Japan, and Canada, are considering data-sharing arrangements between vehicle manufacturers, insurers, and other stakeholders.

---

[7] It should be noted that each of these countries has a stronger social safety net than the United States has, including more-widespread access to medical insurance, which may explain why there is less reliance on litigation to make victims whole following an accident.

How important is consumer acceptance to the deployment of AVs? When we asked experts about the importance of consumer acceptance of AVs, they all responded that it was "very important." An OEM expert stated,

> Consumer acceptance will be critical to the technology. If consumers don't think that the technology can get them from point A to point B, all the resources that have been invested will be wasted. The safe deployment of these vehicles in the public is the best way to show the public that these are safe and reliable ways to get around.

Recent survey research by J. D. Power and Miller Canfield underscored the importance of education by the auto industry about AV capabilities in promoting consumer acceptance. Consumer acceptance appears to be an important factor in the widespread adoption and deployment of AVs. The pace of consumer acceptance of AVs may affect the need to adapt the existing auto insurance framework or adopt a new one.

Will data-sharing between OEMs that produce AVs and insurance companies be important in the future? Currently, there is no established framework for OEMs to provide data on insurance claims to auto insurance providers, although insurance companies contend that they need access to these data to pay claims and assess the risks posed by AVs.[8] Given the lack of clarity about AV data-sharing and its importance to the development of AVs, federal regulators are monitoring the issue in the AV industry. If necessary, they could seek to facilitate data-sharing. Meanwhile, U.S. cities and local transit agencies are actively exploring ways to encourage the sharing of AV data. Although there is no current consensus on a way forward for AV data-sharing between vehicle owners, manufacturers, regulators, and the insurance industry, there are ongoing efforts to address this issue. Although assessing collection and sharing of AV data exceeds the scope of this report, our interviews confirmed that the development of standards for collection and sharing of AV data among stakeholders is an important topic for further research.

We conclude this report with three recommendations:

- **Insurers, manufacturers, and other stakeholders should collaborate to develop a framework for collecting and sharing data on AVs.** Further research to explore methods for information-sharing between insurers and manufacturers could assist the auto insurance industry in more accurately assessing risk, paying claims, creating new insurance products, and facilitating the adoption of AVs.
- **In adapting existing insurance frameworks to accommodate the deployment of AVs, policymakers and insurers in the United States should con-**

---

[8]   As one insurance expert noted in correspondence to the authors on March 18, 2020, "[T]his refers to losses, accidents or malfunctions, because there are no insurance claims unless/until policies are issued—and policies aren't issued unless/until the premium is established, dependent on loss/accident data or other relevant proxies."

sider international insurance frameworks. As discussed in detail in the report, policymakers in the UK, Canada, Japan, Australia, and other countries must also contend with the liability and regulatory implications of the deployment of AVs. Policymakers and insurers in the United States should closely examine these international models, which may provide novel solutions to common liability, coverage, and other issues associated with AVs.

- **Researchers should evaluate the possible effect that the fleet operator model could have on consumer acceptance of vehicles that incorporate technologies that permit autonomous operation at all times.** Further research to understand whether and how the fleet operator model is likely to help or hinder consumer acceptance would be useful. Insurance coverage for AVs in different aspects, such as fleet insurance, will play an important role in increasing consumer confidence in these new technologies. Consumer acceptance of AVs will be an important factor in setting the pace for creation of new or adaptive auto insurance frameworks.

Acknowledgments

We would like to thank the many experts we interviewed throughout the course of this study, without whom the exchange of ideas documented here would not have been possible. We would also like to thank our sponsors, the RAND Institute for Civil Justice, the American Insurance Association (now the American Property Casualty Insurance Association), and The Travelers Companies, for their generous support of the study. We would also like to recognize members of the Institute for Civil Justice Board of Advisors for suggesting the idea of the study. Many organizations have provided experts for our research, and we would like to recognize and thank the following: the American Association for Justice, the American Association of Motor Vehicle Administrators, the American Insurance Association (now the American Property Casualty Insurance Association), the American Trucking Associations, the Association of British Insurers, AXA UK, the Centre for Connected and Autonomous Vehicles, the Consumer Federation of America, Consumer Reports, Ford Motor Company, General Motors, the Insurance Bureau of Canada, ITS America, ITS Japan, Sonja Larkin-Thorne (former consumer advocate, National Association of Insurance Commissioners), Liberty Mutual Insurance, Munich Re, Australia's National Transport Commission, Paulson and Nace, Peloton, Richard Bishop (Bishop Consulting), Santa Clara University School of Law, the Shared-Use Mobility Center, Steven Shladover (University of California Partners for Advanced Transportation Technology program), Slavik Law Firm, Bryant Walker Smith (University of South Carolina), State Farm Mutual Automobile Insurance Company, Swiss Re, Tesla, Travelers, Uber, the UK Department for Transport, the UK Law Commission, the U.S. Department of Transportation, and Zoox. We also wish to thank the peer reviewers of this report and members of the Institute for Civil Justice Board of Advisors for their thoughtful suggestions. The report is much improved as a result of their labors.

We note that the views expressed in the report represent the perspectives of the various individuals we interviewed and do not necessarily reflect the views of their employers or of the sponsors of the study.

Abbreviations

ADS	automated driving system
AEVA	Automated and Electric Vehicles Act 2018 (United Kingdom)
AV	autonomous vehicle
GPS	Global Positioning System
IBC	Insurance Bureau of Canada
MAII	motor accident injury insurance
MLIT	Ministry of Land, Infrastructure, Transport and Tourism (Japan)
NHTSA	National Highway Traffic Safety Administration
NIIS	National Injury Insurance Scheme (Australia)
NTC	National Transport Commission (Australia)
OEM	original equipment manufacturer
SAE	Society of Automotive Engineers
UK	United Kingdom

CHAPTER ONE

Introduction

Automobile insurance is an important consideration in the deployment of vehicles that incorporate technologies that will permit autonomous operation at all or most times, and it is therefore a critical factor that policymakers must consider as they seek to realize the societal benefits of automation. This is true both from the standpoint of compliance with existing state regulations and from the perspective of consumer confidence in these new technologies. From a regulatory perspective, policymakers wish to ensure compensation for those involved in automobile accidents. Original equipment manufacturers (OEMs) may consider bundling insurance as part of the sale of an autonomous vehicle (AV), to indicate confidence in its technologies. Insurance can serve to assure the public that AVs are safe and that any mishaps will be compensated. Until consumers are convinced that AVs are safe, deployment of vehicles that are capable of autonomous operation might be slow, despite the tremendous investments made by OEMs and related companies. Failure to inspire consumer confidence in AV technologies could result in market failure and the loss of the social benefits of these technologies (Anderson, Kalra, Stanley, Sorensen, et al., 2016).

The potential benefits of AV technologies are significant. Most important is that AVs have the potential to save lives and prevent injuries. Currently, conventional car crashes cause approximately 4.5 million injuries and 36,560 fatalities per year in the United States (National Highway Traffic Safety Administration [NHTSA], 2019; National Safety Council, undated). For the National Motor Vehicle Crash Causation Survey, researchers studied crashes from a two-year period. They determined that "[t]he critical reason, which is the last event in the crash causal chain, was assigned to the driver in 94 percent (±2.2%) of the crashes" (NHTSA, 2015, p. 1). In 2016, NHTSA stated that it was working to "address the human choices that are linked to 94 percent of serious crashes" (NHTSA, 2017). NHTSA also stated that it

> continues to promote vehicle technologies that hold the potential to reduce the number of crashes and save thousands of lives every year, and may eventually help reduce or eliminate human error and the mistakes that drivers make behind the wheel.

First, we define some key terms. NHTSA has adopted a system created by the Society of Automotive Engineers (SAE) to describe the levels of vehicle automation. The scale goes from 0 (no automation) to 5 (full automation) (NHTSA, undated a). Vehicles operating at Level 0, 1, 2, or 3 we call *automated*. In this report, we discuss vehicles we call *autonomous*—those that operate at SAE Level 4 or 5:

- At **Level 4**, or **high automation**, "[a]n automated driving system (ADS) on the vehicle can itself perform all driving tasks and monitor the driving environment—essentially, do all the driving—in *certain* circumstances. The human need not pay attention in those circumstances" (NHTSA, undated a; emphasis ours).
- At **Level 5**, or **full automation**, "[a]n automated driving system (ADS) on the vehicle can do all the driving in *all* circumstances. The human occupants are just passengers and need never be involved in driving" (NHTSA, undated a; emphasis ours).

Although even simple forms of automation (e.g., automatic emergency braking) offer significant safety benefits, many of the benefits of autonomy will be realized once vehicles are able to operate at Levels 4 and 5. There are also considerable social benefits to be realized at Levels 4 and 5, including providing mobility benefits to tens of millions of Americans who cannot drive because of, for example, disability or age; possibly reducing traffic congestion; and improving land use, especially in urban areas. At the same time, however, the introduction of AVs will likely create uncertainty regarding regulation and insurance. The challenge for policymakers is to maximize the benefits associated with AVs while reducing the uncertainty occasioned by their introduction.

Despite the potential benefits of AVs, there are substantial challenges to their deployment. These challenges include various technological barriers. For example, it is difficult for the sensors and cameras in today's automated vehicles to perform well in certain weather conditions, including snow, black ice, and dust. In addition, many roads in the United States are unpaved and lack the signage, markings, and mapping needed to enable most AVs to safely navigate them. How conventional vehicles perform in these conditions is unlikely to be a good predictor for the performance of vehicles with Level 4 and Level 5 capabilities, so the insurance industry will need to develop and adapt risk factors for AVs.

Other challenges include existing uncertainty surrounding the business models that will be employed to support the broader deployment of AVs, in that these vehicles may be significantly more expensive than conventional cars and will require specific maintenance to ensure that their safety features are working properly. Some OEMs plan to lease their AVs as part of fleets rather than to sell them individually, at least at first. In another potential model, an AV would have a separate owner, such as an OEM; an operator, such as a grocery chain or food delivery service; and a maintenance company responsible for ensuring the vehicle's continued safe operation. One of the aspects of our study has been to explore how these new business models could affect automobile insurance.

Other challenges include the lack of federal safety standards for AVs and the absence of a common set of regulations that apply throughout the United States. Currently, there are additional crash event data recorder requirements for AVs in some states, such as Nevada (Anderson, Kalra, Stanley, Sorensen, et al., 2016). Having separate state-by-state requirements could complicate the mass production of AVs. As indicated previously, without consumer acceptance, the AV market could fail (Anderson, Kalra, Stanley, Sorensen, et al., 2016).

The research questions that we explored were the following:

- Will the introduction of AVs that have Level 4 or 5 capabilities require significant changes to the existing U.S. automobile insurance system, or is the current insurance model flexible enough to handle vehicles that incorporate technologies that permit autonomous operation at most or all times?
- What are the benefits and drawbacks of potential future models for automobile insurance?
- What is the likelihood that AVs will be insured in fleets rather than by individual policy holders?
- Is the subrogation process likely to change in future models for automobile insurance?
- In the future, how might accidents between AVs and conventional vehicles and between AVs and pedestrians be handled?
- Will minor accidents and "fender benders" become significantly more costly due to the cost of repairing the sensors in AVs, or is this concern overblown?
- How might changes to accommodate AVs in the insurance models of other countries inform changes to U.S. automobile insurance?
- How important is consumer acceptance for the deployment of AVs?

As our research developed, we also explored the following question:

- Will data-sharing between OEMs and insurance companies be important in the future?

Methodology

To investigate the potential impact that the introduction of AVs could have on the U.S. automobile insurance industry, we conducted semistructured interviews with a broad variety of stakeholders, including representatives from automobile insurance companies, manufacturers, state and federal government, consumer advocacy groups, ridesharing companies, AV and trucking start-ups, industry associations, and academia.

We also interviewed plaintiff's lawyers and defense lawyers who practice in this field. Finally, we interviewed experts and regulators in Japan, Australia, Canada, and the United Kingdom (UK). We selected these countries because compensating the injured is a guiding principle of their auto insurance frameworks. This approach, which supplemented a literature review, was undertaken as the best method to obtain candid assessments from a wide variety of subject-matter experts. The purpose of this study was to explore experts' current thinking about the potential impact that AVs could have on the automobile insurance industry and on future insurance models. We were able to interview experts who possess personal experience with developing insurance models, AV regulatory policies, and AV business models and technology, among other related topics. The interviews allowed in-depth discussion of the assessments that the experts provided, in contrast to the constraints of a survey model.

Specifically, we invited 38 participants to be interviewed for the study. Thirty-five organizations agreed to be interviewed, which included a total of 43 subject-matter experts; three prospective participants declined our requests for interviews. The interviews were conducted via phone by one or more authors of this report between October 2018 and June 2019. Participants were identified based on their prior and current engagement with issues relevant to the insurance implications of AVs. Participants were selected to provide perspectives on the impact that AVs could have on the U.S. insurance industry, as well as several foreign insurance markets. The semistructured protocol allowed us to elicit the participants' expert opinions in a way that allowed for both consistency, based on a set of common questions that all participants were asked to answer, and flexibility, whereby interviews could focus on specific topics based on the particular expertise and perspective of the participant. The protocol included the following questions:

1. What might be the models for insuring AVs in the future?
2. If fleet ownership becomes popular for AVs, how might collision claims be handled?
3. How do you view the importance of consumer acceptance of AVs?
4. How might AVs change the subrogation of auto insurance claims?
5. How might small accidents and fender benders for AVs be handled?
6. How might accidents between AVs and conventional cars be handled? What about accidents involving AVs and pedestrians or bikes?
7. Would a [state] no-fault approach (similar to existing no-fault auto insurance) be attractive?
8. Would a national statutory no-fault model be attractive?
9. Is it likely that property damage coverage will remain the same?
10. What is wrong—if anything—with our current auto insurance system?
11. Do you have any other suggestions or comments about other anticipated changes to the automobile insurance industry?

We created a matrix of stakeholder perspectives on these discrete issues to assess the extent to which stakeholders anticipated that the insurance industry might change and the popularity of different insurance models.

In the report, we handle the wide variety of expert opinions on these topics in two ways: (1) We describe variation in expert perspectives, and (2) we describe how different stakeholders are preparing for the future deployment and widespread adoption of AVs. In addition, we characterize which perspectives were most popular among stakeholders.

The limitations of this approach include the inherent difficulty of predicting the future impact that AVs could have on the insurance industry, given existing uncertainty about the capabilities and timeline for deployment of these technologies. It is difficult to model the risks posed by the AVs of the future, which makes it challenging for stakeholders to assess the feasibility of various insurance models.

Structure of This Report

Following this introduction, in Chapter Two, we explore tort law in theory and in practice, focusing on how tort law may adapt to—or facilitate—the introduction of AVs. To provide theoretical context for the remainder of the report, we review key tort law principles and the three central justifications for tort law. In Chapter Three, we examine a variety of potential future models for the automobile insurance industry. These models include adapting the existing auto insurance framework, national no-fault insurance, state no-fault insurance, manufacturer self-insurance, and fleet ownership policies. In Chapter Four, we address different automobile insurance models for AVs in the UK, Japan, Canada, and Australia and explain how these models may inform future reforms of the U.S. automobile insurance industry. In Chapter Five, we explore key risks associated with AVs, including software updates, the cost of sensors, cybersecurity, remote operators, data-sharing, and consumer acceptance and report how stakeholders suggest that the U.S. automobile insurance industry may handle these risks. Finally, in Chapter Six, we outline our findings and offer several recommendations. We also include an appendix supporting the information in Chapter Four.

CHAPTER TWO

Tort Law and Autonomous Vehicles, in Theory and Practice

In this chapter, we consider the effect that AVs have on liability and insurance and the basis for compensating people injured in accidents involving AVs. To do so, it will be helpful to start with first principles. Liability for damage to others makes up the largest portion of most automobile insurance policies, so we need to closely examine what might create those liabilities. To do this, we need to examine the fundamentals of tort law—the law of private wrongs. What is the purpose of the tort law system? And what does that tell us about how automation may change automobile insurance?

Historically, the three primary theoretical justifications for tort law (including products liability) have been (1) deterrence, (2) corrective justice or civil recourse, and (3) compensation (American Law Institute, 1979, § 901). In this chapter, we briefly review each justification and explain why, *in theory*, an increase in automation is likely to increase the liability of the manufacturer and decrease the liability of the individual driver. In the next section of this chapter, we discuss auto tort *in practice*, the considerable gap between theory and practice, and why existing models of auto insurance are likely to remain relevant.

In addition, although all manufacturers of passenger vehicles are gradually adding more automated features, it is likely that initial deployments of Levels 4 and 5 of these technologies will not occur in individually owned and operated private vehicles but rather in fleets of commercially owned and operated vehicles, which have a substantially different insurance market. We therefore also consider the difference between individual and fleet owners and how that affects insurers.

Our analysis is primarily descriptive (describing what we think the law *will* be) rather than normative (opining about what the law *should* be). We describe why we think the courts are likely to make the decisions that they will. As in many legal analyses, this necessarily requires an examination of the normative justifications for the courts' decisions and whether we think they are likely to prevail. This requires some normative analysis to predict what courts are likely to decide. But the primary objective of our analysis is descriptive rather than normative.

Deterrence

A critical justification for the tort system is its role in deterring wrongdoing. Imposing the costs of wrongful actions on the wrongdoer creates incentives for the wrongdoer to avoid these actions or take precautions to reduce harm. So, for example, the likelihood of being held liable for harm to a pedestrian if, for instance, a driver negligently runs a red light increases the driver's incentive to drive safely. Similarly, if a manufacturer makes widgets with defects that might make the widgets unreasonably likely to injure someone, the liability costs that the manufacturer would incur for selling these defective widgets would create incentives for quality control and decreasing the production of defective widgets.[1]

Producing dangerous products or undertaking risky action can be viewed as creating what economists call a *negative externality*—an action that imposes a cost on others besides those reflected in the price. By making the tortfeasor liable, tort law can help, *at least in theory*, internalize that externality—making sure that the actor imposing the cost also bears that cost.

Although the idea that tort law deters misconduct has long existed, judges Richard Posner and Guido Calabresi helped develop and popularize an economic version of this conception and justification for tort law (Calabresi, 1970; Landes and Posner, 1987). Judge Calabresi argued that economic efficiency dictated that courts should generally place liability on the "cheapest cost avoider"—the party in the best position to minimize net accident costs.[2]

Historically, one could argue that, in the case of automobile crashes, the individual driver was the party in the best position to reduce accident costs. The driver directly controlled every operation of the vehicle, its location, the conditions of the driving, whether to go on safer or more-dangerous roads, speed, and the attention that was being paid to the driving task at any given time.[3]

Even as far back as 1970, when AVs were quite far from becoming a reality, Calabresi suggested that the car manufacturer might actually be the cheapest cost avoider and could control many important causes of accidents and the harms that the individual driver could not. So, for example, the manufacturer could control the maximum

---

[1]   Of course, tort law is not the only set of incentives that actors face. Regulation, criminal law, and market pressures also create incentives that affect drivers, manufacturers, and fleet operators.

[2]   Oliver Wendell Holmes made a similar point, but one focused on ensuring safety rather than efficiency: "[T]he safest way to secure care is to throw the risk upon the person who decides what precautions shall be taken" (Holmes, 1881, p. 117).

Modern traffic safety researchers use the term *crash* instead of *accident* in part to emphasize the fact that these incidents are the result of specific decisions and not unavoidable. However, much of the legal literature predates the adoption of this term and uses the term *accident*. In this report, we use *crash* and *accident* interchangeably.

[3]   In reality, of course, accident costs are likely to be reduced by the decisions of a multitude of actors, so the optimal system gives multiple actors incentives to reduce accident costs. Various tort law doctrines exist that have the effect of making liability uncertain and thereby spreading these incentives. See generally Anderson, 2007.

speed of the vehicle and how dangerous it was to pedestrians and other vehicles as a result of design decisions about, for example, its shape and mass, seatbelts, and airbags. If these factors were more determinative of accidents than actions of the driver were, he suggested, auto manufacturers might actually be the cheapest cost avoiders, even in conventional vehicles with no automation (Level 0) (Calabresi, 1970).

In any event, automation makes it more likely that the "driver" is not the "cheapest cost avoider." The fact that the human driver does less and the automation more weakens the rationale of imposing liability on the driver in the hope of creating incentives to reduce accident costs. The car is doing more and the driver less. This is particularly true at Level 4 or 5, when the automation has assumed the dynamic driving task and the human driver has, by definition, no control over how the automation executes the driving task. Or to put it another way, little deterrence is created by placing liability on the driver if the driver (or, more precisely, the user) has no control over the factors that create crashes or accidents.

The manufacturer can control the speed and driving characteristics of the vehicle and the way it reacts to other vehicles and environmental hazards in a way that most efficiently balances safety with transportation efficiency. For this reason, the deterrence justification in tort law probably suggests increased liability on the part of those parties best able to control the automation, the vehicle design, and its integration, which is, most likely, the manufacturer, as opposed to the individual driver. Thus, we might expect that the number or dollar value (or both) of successful products liability lawsuits against the manufacturer in the wake of crashes will increase and successful suits against individual drivers will decrease.

On one theory, it does not matter whether courts decide that the driver or the manufacturer is more liable. Ronald Coase noted that, with the critical assumption of no transaction costs, it did not matter whether liability was placed on the cheapest cost avoider because, if liability were placed on the wrong party, that party would pay the cheapest cost avoider to take whatever accident reduction methods were cost justified (Coase, 1960). For example, imagine that the most efficient way of reducing manufacturing defects in cars was under the manufacturer's control but that the legislature imposed liability onto dealerships for damage incurred because of defects in cars. Dealerships would have an incentive to contract with manufacturers to undertake this defect reduction method simply to decrease the dealerships' likely liability. Similarly, if drivers retained primary liability but manufacturers were in the best position to reduce accident costs, drivers might choose to purchase vehicles from only the safest manufacturers and willingly (and efficiently) pay extra for safer vehicles. But Coase's assumption of no transaction costs is a heroic one, and, absent compelling counterarguments, economic analysis would suggest reducing the human driver's liability as the driver's role in avoiding crashes reduces.

The economic question as to whether the manufacturer or driver should be liable may be more difficult to answer with respect to a fleet owner-operator who has substantial control over the operation of the fleet of vehicles.[4] In this case, the ultimate degree of liability may depend on the causal factors that lead to the particular crash. If, for example, the fleet owner-operator deliberately used the vehicles in inclement weather outside the manufacturer's designated parameters for safe operation of the vehicle (the vehicle's operational design domain), the fleet operator may be the most efficient cost-avoider.[5] In contrast, if the fleet owner-operator was employing the AVs in accordance with the manufacturer's guidelines but the vehicle still crashed, the manufacturer would be in the best position to undertake efficient safety precautions.[6]

Corrective Justice or Civil Recourse

Another key justification of tort law focuses on corrective justice and civil recourse. Although these theories are distinct, they share a focus on the ethical foundations of tort law and personal responsibility. The corrective justice justification of tort law focuses on tort law as a means of achieving corrective justice (in contrast with distributive justice) by righting a particular wrong and emphasizing a duty to repair (Weinrib, 2012; Wells, 1990; Coleman, 2001).[7] Civil recourse theory suggests that tort law provides a procedural mechanism to seek redress in a civil society for a wrong. In the words of one of its leading proponents, "The principle of civil recourse is simply that an individual who has been legally wronged is entitled to some avenue of recourse against the one who wronged her" (Zipursky, 2003, p. 754). In either case, the focus is on the tortfeasor's moral personal responsibility to the injured party.

As was the case with deterrence (and for somewhat similar reasons), we anticipate that the increase of automation will change defendants' relative moral culpability. It is harder to view the individual driver as morally culpable for a crash if the driver is rea-

---

[4]   In this discussion, we presume that the fleet operator either purchases or leases the vehicles from the manufacturer. Other arrangements are possible. Tesla, for example, has suggested that individual owners of its vehicles could earn money by leasing them out as fully automated robotaxis when they were not being used by the owners. The liability implications of such an arrangement could be complex, but, absent specific contractual provisions to the contrary, liability would likely fall on the manufacturer because it is likely the party in the best position to reduce net accident costs.

[5]   An automated vehicle's operational design domain is a description of the specific operating domain or domains in which an automated function or system is designed to properly operate, such as roadway types, speed range, and environmental conditions (e.g., weather, daytime versus nighttime).

[6]   As noted in Kalra, Anderson, and Wachs, 2009, and Marchant and Lindor, 2012, this shift in liability could theoretically slow manufacturers' willingness to adopt these technologies.

[7]   Aristotle distinguished distributive justice from corrective justice in *Nicomachean Ethics*, Book V (Aristotle, 350 BCE, Chapter 4). Distributive justice addresses the overall distribution of resources in a society. In contrast, corrective justice focuses on justice between two individuals in the wake of a harm that one causes to another.

sonably relying on automation to conduct the driving task.[8] And although it may be psychologically easier to impute moral responsibility to another human being than to an organization, it is likely that the entity responsible for the automation will also be seen as possessing the relevant moral responsibility. For individually operated vehicles, this entity is likely to be the manufacturer. Indeed, the public's moral revulsion at an automated vehicle that runs someone over by mistake may be greater than that for an individual human driver doing so.

As was the case with deterrence, fleet operation may complicate the analysis and the question of relative responsibility may be less clear.[9] In the event of a crash, what moral duty is owed to the injured, and by whom? Imagine that person A hires a robotaxi from company X and directs it to take her to work. If the vehicle malfunctions and runs over a pedestrian on the route, who is morally responsible? It seems unlikely to be person A, who did not, in this hypothetical, undertake any act that would conventionally be thought blameworthy. If the vehicle were being operated reasonably by the fleet operator, the most morally responsible entity may be the manufacturer that designed the vehicle.

Compensation

In this view, tort law exists primarily to compensate the injured. The focus is not so much on deterring misconduct or achieving corrective justice by righting wrongs but primarily on compensating victims.[10] Tort law serves, in this view, an insurance function by spreading losses that would be very burdensome for an individual across many, making compensating those losses less burdensome.

This rationale also supports a shift in liability from the individual driver to the manufacturer. Manufacturers are simply better able to bear the costs of a serious injury than an individual driver would be. Although most individual drivers now have insur-

---

[8] Corrective justice theorists often cite intentional torts as exemplars. Jules Coleman, for example, emphasized assault and battery as a paradigmatic example of a wrong that creates a duty of repair (Coleman, 2001).

[9] Historically, common carriers—that is, companies regularly transporting people or goods—have had a heightened duty of care toward passengers.

[10] See, for example, Justice Roger Traynor's statement in *Escola v. Coca-Cola Bottling Co.*, 150 P.2d 436 (Cal. 1944), that

> [t]he cost of an injury and the loss of time or health may be an overwhelming misfortune to the person injured, and a needless one, for the risk of injury can be insured by the manufacturer and distributed among the public as a cost of doing business. (150 P.2d at 441)

Fleming James is perhaps most associated with this justification. See Priest, 1985. When this rationale was most avidly forwarded, fewer were covered by medical insurance, so tort liability played a larger role in covering medical bills than it does today. As medical insurance has become more common, this rationale may have lost some of its force.

ance, the policy limits of those insurance policies are often very low—far less than the medical costs incurred because of a serious accident (Anderson, Heaton, and Carroll, 2010).

In the case of a fleet operator with commercial insurance, however, the compensation rationale may suggest making the operator rather than the manufacturer primarily responsible. In most cases, fleet operators are likely to have to comply with either Federal Motor Carrier Safety Administration requirements for liability insurance or analogous state provisions, and the required liability insurance is relatively large and far more likely to cover injuries than individual drivers' insurance would be. To the extent that fleets are permitted to legally operate without such liability insurance, the compensation rationale would suggest shifting liability to manufacturers.

Automobile Tort Law in Practice

As explained earlier, there are theoretical reasons to anticipate that an increase in vehicle automation will lead to a decrease in individual driver liability and an increase in vehicle manufacturer liability. But Oliver Wendell Holmes famously observed that "[t]he life of the law has not been logic: it has been experience" (Holmes, 1881, p. 1), and the actual daily practice of automobile tort law suggests that, notwithstanding the logical theoretical reasons for anticipating a shift in liability from individual drivers toward manufacturers as automation increases, that shift may be gradual and mediated by the existing U.S. system of compensation for automobile crashes.

Even today, there is a substantial gap between the tort law one learns in law school and the actual practice of automotive law (Baker, 2001). In theory, every automobile fender bender could be litigated. But in practice, automobile law has become a large administrative system operated by insurers. The vast majority of incidents are resolved quickly and relatively efficiently. Lawsuits, to say nothing of actual trials, are exceedingly rare. Rules of thumb (e.g., the car that rear-ends another is always at fault) are used instead of searching inquiries into the reasonableness of a particular driver's or manufacturer's actions. Disputes as to whom is at fault among insurance companies are typically resolved in arbitration (Anderson, Heaton, and Carroll, 2010; Engstrom, 2012; Engstrom, 2018).

Similarly, it is rare for parties other than motorists to be sued. From a theoretical perspective, a car crash can be the result of many causal factors, including road design, lighting, speed limits, the design of the vehicle, the decision to purchase a particular vehicle, or even the decision to drive. The list of potential defendants could include the city, county, state, and federal governments, in addition to the road designer, OEM, and, depending on the facts of the crash, still others (Anderson, 2007).

Yet, despite this theoretical range of potential defendants (some well-resourced), people rarely seek compensation from anyone other than the other driver's insurance company (Engstrom, 2011). In very serious cases, the manufacturers may be sued, but those are rare cases, typically involving very serious injuries. This is partly due to social convention—the public is accustomed to blaming drivers for crashes—not the fact that vehicles are designed in a particular way.[11]

These social conventions are not likely to evaporate overnight. The public is accustomed to blaming the driver—not the manufacturer—of the other vehicle. And if automation is introduced gradually—if the capacity of vehicles for self-driving grows slowly over various operational design domains—the human driver may still have a significant role and involvement in the operation of the vehicle for some time to come. There are also significant reasons to anticipate some variation of the existing legal system for some time, for reasons of both claim administration and underwriting.

The existing infrastructure for handling crashes is likely to resist change. This is partly due to sheer volume. In a typical year in the United States, there are more than 6.3 million police-reported crashes (NHTSA, 2016) and more than 4.6 million injuries from car crashes (Statistics Department, 2018). This volume of potentially tortious events requires a vast infrastructure of claim adjusters to process, adjudicate, and resolve the claims.

Suppose that an automated vehicle collides with a human-driven one, resulting in minor damage, as happens thousands of times every day. As noted above, there are theoretical reasons to anticipate that manufacturers may bear more of these costs as the human takes on less of the driving function, but, as a practical matter, manufacturers lack an infrastructure to address so many minor claims. They lack a network of claim adjusters, relationships with body shops, arbitrators, and lawyers—a vast skilled workforce whose primary function is to resolve the enormous volume of minor crashes. Even if automation dramatically reduces the incidence of at-fault crashes by avoiding human error, there are likely to be many crashes that still involve human-driven vehicles that will need to be resolved.

There are also many auto claims (e.g., hail damage, tree limbs, broken window from theft) that have nothing to do with the operation of the vehicle. Presumably, even if manufacturers were strictly liable for all mishaps caused by vehicle operation, individual vehicle owners may still need to retain coverage for such occurrences of property damage. This may create additional inertia in the existing U.S. insurance model.

As noted above, automation may be first introduced in large fleets of robotaxis that are operated by third parties. Large fleet operators are better positioned than manufacturers to resolve claims, but it is unlikely that they have the particular expertise that insurers have to efficiently resolve claims.

With respect to underwriting, automation may make the human driver far less important. The enormous expertise possessed by insurers to price insurance efficiently

---

[11] See Geistfeld, 2017 (noting logical rationale of tort suit against sport-utility vehicles for additional hazard they cause); Elish, 2019; and Anderson, 2007 (noting numerous logical causes of crashes).

in a way to allocate risk becomes potentially far less valuable in a world in which the vehicle characteristics supplant driver characteristics as primary determinants of risk. As automation becomes a more important factor in determining risk than human behavior is, the manufacturer may be better positioned to collect the information necessary to underwrite efficiently. Even if humans are playing a significant role in the driving function, manufacturers may be able to more easily collect rich data on human driving behavior and the sources of risk than insurers are. Manufacturers, however, lack experience in navigating the state-based insurance regulatory system with 50 different legal regimes. This may be a significant impediment to offering competing insurance products.

At least currently, manufacturers also lack the same relationship with the customer that insurance companies have cultivated. Insurers have attempted to develop brands of being dependable partners in troubled times. "Like a Good Neighbor," "The Rock," "The Good Hands People"—each motto speaks of an effort in branding to develop a level of trust. In many cases, the primary contact is a local independent insurance agent who may provide a range of insurance products in addition to vehicle insurance. Insurers have attempted to develop a relationship with customers with respect to this service that may provide an additional friction to a wholesale reorganization of the process for compensating individuals for automobile crashes, at least with respect to individually owned and operated vehicles.

There are also practical legal obstacles to filing a lawsuit against a manufacturer. Although suits against individual drivers usually allege simple negligence, based on the facts of the crash, suits against manufacturers in products liability typically allege a manufacturing design, a design defect, or failure to warn.[12] Each typically involves a significant burden of proof to show that the manufacturer did not meet the appropriate legal standard. Although a plaintiff could attempt to show that such fault on the part of the manufacturer can be inferred solely from the circumstances of the crash, most auto products liability cases today involve numerous experts and are therefore expensive and complicated to litigate.

Owners of fleets of AVs may be in a good position to contract with commercial insurers to provide adequate insurance. They may be large enough to develop sufficient internal expertise in handling claims or may contract with insurers with this expertise. From an underwriting perspective, they may also have sufficient data to allow an insurer to calculate appropriate risk premiums, particularly if the primary determinant of those premiums is the vehicle rather than the driver.

---

[12] See, generally, Anderson, Kalra, Stanley, Sorensen, et al., 2016, pp. 118–126, for discussion of products liability for automated vehicles.

For insurers of both individuals and fleets, subrogation is also likely to play a significant role in shifting the ultimate burden of liability.[13] In this context, the insurer of either a privately owned auto or a fleet operator can seek subrogation from the manufacturer because automation makes the manufacturer more responsible, as discussed above. In this way, the ultimate liability may be shifted onto the manufacturer despite the continuation of the existing automobile insurance law infrastructure. If this occurs, the consumer-facing aspects of insurance are likely to remain the same. Owners of vehicles would still obtain insurance from conventional auto insurers, which would still pay claims. But the proportion of subrogation claims that insurers would file against manufacturers might rise appreciably. Depending on the volume of claims, this might have the long-term effect of decreasing the cost of automobile insurance but increasing the costs of the vehicles themselves. However, one of the key promises of automation is that an automated vehicle would be significantly less likely to crash than human drivers are, or so one would hope, so the overall number and value of crashes would significantly decline.

A similar dynamic might occur in the robotaxi fleet context. Commercial insurers of the fleets would pay individual claims but might file subrogation claims against manufacturers more frequently.

Conclusion

From a theoretical perspective, there are several reasons to think that automation will lead to a shift in liability from the individual driver (and the driver's insurer) to the manufacturer. The primary historical justifications of tort law offer a few rationales for such a shift. Existing products liability law doctrines, including manufacturing defect, design defect, and failure to warn, could readily apply to crashes involving automated vehicles. Indeed, products liability's doctrinal focus on design defects and failure to warn is arguably more relevant to such a crash than an analysis would be that focuses on driver performance. To be clear, this is a descriptive prediction of how courts and legal analysts are likely to apply the predominant justifications of tort law to these new technologies and not a normative argument either in favor of or against such an approach. For fleet operators, it is also likely that there will be a shift toward manufacturer liability, although the question is more complex.

There are numerous practical reasons, however, to think that this shift toward manufacturer liability will be more gradual. The sheer volume of auto crashes requires a vast infrastructure of specialists who resolve, adjudicate, and repair the damage from

---

[13] Subrogation is a defendant's ability to seek recovery from another party. So, if plaintiff A successfully recovers payment from defendant X, defendant X can then sue defendant Y. For example, suppose that a plaintiff successfully recovered payment from a defendant driver's auto insurance company. That auto insurance company might be able to sue the OEM if it felt that the legal responsibility ultimately rested at the OEM's feet.

these claims. And although one hopes that increased automation will lead to fewer crashes, this transition is likely to be gradual. Insurers have considerable specialized expertise in this role. It is unlikely that manufacturers will replicate this infrastructure overnight or that people will soon view products liability suits against manufacturers as the obvious mechanism for resolving a minor crash.

It seems likely that manufacturers may increasingly compete with traditional auto insurers and offer insurance packaged with their vehicles. Tesla, for example, has announced that it will do so (Moorcraft, 2019).[14] To the extent that the primary determinants of crashes are vehicle characteristics rather than driver characteristics, manufacturers may, in fact, be in a better position to collect data and underwrite the risks as efficiently as possible. Similarly, if automation dramatically reduces claim frequency, it may reduce the scale of infrastructure necessary. Insurance bundled with the price of the vehicle may be an attractive concept for some consumers. But it is also possible that manufacturers will decide that underwriting, regulatory compliance, and handling of claims are outside their core competencies and either outsource those functions or leave insurance products to insurers.

Operators of fleets of automated vehicles may also serve an important role as providers of insured transportation. They may self-insure and have the size and expertise to subrogate claims against manufacturers when appropriate.[15] It is possible that, if more consumers decide that private car ownership is not necessary or worth the inconvenience, such fleets will decrease the rate of private car ownership. This would, of course, reduce the demand for private auto insurance.

Policymakers do not need to fundamentally change automobile insurance law to see automated vehicle technology advance. Currently, insurance is governed by states, and each state sets its own particular requirements and requires rate approval. This makes some sense in the federal system because tort law is primarily a function of state law. This also permits a state-by-state determination of financial solvency and rates.[16]

At some point, there could be tension over data. Currently, the most-relevant data for determining crash risks are based on past human behavior, are possessed by insurers, and are used by state regulatory authorities for solvency and rate approval. As automation supplants human behavior in the dynamic driving task, these data become less relevant. The data that become more relevant in determining risks are about the

---

[14] Tesla partnered with State National Insurance to provide this insurance. Earlier, Tesla had partnered with Liberty Mutual and Aviva.

[15] One stakeholder noted, "They may be obligated to self-insure up to higher than anticipated retentions, based on the fact that there is no data on which insurers can appropriately price liability policies."

[16] The state-by-state insurance system does pose a significant burden to new entrants wanting to offer new insurance products. If policymakers wanted to increase competition and potentially permit new entrants, they could consider a federal insurance charter so that an insurer would have to clear only one set of federal regulatory barriers to offer insurance in the country, or policymakers could consider liberalizing and standardizing state-by-state requirements. But this would require a substantial revision to existing insurance law.

functioning of the automation and are likely to be possessed by manufacturers, which are not currently part of the solvency and rate-setting regulatory process.

In this chapter, we examined the predominant justifications for tort law—deterrence, corrective justice or civil recourse, and compensation—and their likely implications for auto liability. We contrasted automobile tort law in theory with automobile tort law in practice. In Chapter Three, we examine how the deployment of AVs may affect future insurance models.

CHAPTER THREE

Stakeholder Assessments of Models for Insuring Autonomous Vehicles

In this chapter, we consider how the deployment of AVs could affect future insurance models. As AV technologies advance in coming decades, it will be necessary to carefully consider how liability and insurance are treated. We drew on both recent scholarship and interviews with key stakeholders. We consider the following future models for insuring AVs:

- national no-fault
- state no-fault
- self-insurance by manufacturers
- fleet insurance policies
- adaptation of the existing automobile insurance framework.

In this chapter, we examine how and why experts ranked the models, beginning with the least likely model and ending with the most probable. Although the experts we interviewed expressed nuanced opinions, even those stakeholders who anticipated changes in the insurance industry thought that the status quo would persist for the foreseeable future. Those insurers who foresaw changes in the industry were split as to whether those changes would occur at Level 3 or 4. One stakeholder captured the majority view by stating, "The existing structure [of the insurance industry] can and will adapt to the different needs of higher levels of automation." To illustrate this perspective, we report the experts' assessments about several automobile claim scenarios and whether they would change significantly if an AV were part of the incident. These claim scenarios are as follows:

- an accident involving an AV and a conventional vehicle
- an accident involving an AV and a pedestrian
- property damage to an AV.

Table 3.1 summarizes U.S. experts' perceptions of the likelihood of success of future U.S. insurance frameworks. Table 3.2 outlines the experts' assessments of the criteria these experts used to assess the likelihood of success of possible future insurance frameworks.

Table 3.1
U.S. Interviewees' Perceptions of the Likelihood of Success of Fleet Insurance, National No-Fault, State No-Fault, and Self-Insurance Models for Autonomous Vehicles

Likelihood of Success	National No-Fault	State No-Fault	Self-Insurance	Fleet Insurance
Likely to succeed	0	23	23	64
Not likely to succeed	73	41		
No response	27	36	77	36
Total	100	100	100	100

NOTE: The data are percentages of the 22 respondents pairing a given likelihood of success with each model (n = 22). We exclude here approximately 12 experts from other countries whom we did not ask about the United States. Each response reflects one interview. Some interviews included multiple participants.

Table 3.2
Experts' Assessments of the Criteria for Assessing the Future Feasibility of Existing and Alternative Insurance Frameworks

Criterion	Existing Framework	Fleet Insurance	National No-Fault	State No-Fault	Self-Insurance
Is legislative action required?	No	No	Yes	No	No
Does it incentivize manufacturer safety?	Yes	Yes	No	No	Yes
What effect would it have on fraud concerns?	No increase	No increase	No increase	May increase	No increase
What effect would it have on the ease of the claims process for the consumer?	Same	Same	Depends on the particulars of the statutory scheme	Easier	Depends on procedures set up by the self-insurer
Does it apply to all levels of autonomy?	Maybe; changes may be needed at Level 3 or 4	Yes	No; it would apply at Levels 4 and 5 only	Yes; it may become more attractive at higher levels of autonomy	Yes

NOTE: Red indicates a negative; dark green indicates a positive. Orange indicates a qualified negative; light green indicates no change or a qualified positive. Yellow indicates uncertainty or mixed results.

Now we provide more detail on each model considered, plus some other variations proposed.

A National No-Fault Insurance Model for Autonomous Vehicles

Our literature review, which included academic and legal perspectives on liability issues relevant to the deployment of AVs, suggested that the introduction of a no-fault compensation scheme may be advisable as AVs become more popular (see, e.g., Pearl, 2019). With this in mind, we consulted stakeholders about two forms of no-fault insurance: (1) the state no-fault auto insurance model employed in 12 U.S. states and Puerto Rico (Robinette, 2020) and (2) a national no-fault insurance model similar to the schemes devised for the nuclear power industry and pharmaceutical companies that produce vaccines. Stakeholders did not view the introduction of a national no-fault insurance system for AVs as a realistic possibility. Although national no-fault schemes have been enacted in the context of injuries stemming from both vaccines and nuclear reactors, stakeholders noted that the AV industry differs considerably from these examples.

The National Vaccine Injury Compensation Program

In November 1986, Congress passed the National Childhood Vaccine Injury Act (Pub. L. No. 99-660, Title III, as codified at 42 U.S.C. §§ 300aa-10–300aa-33). The act established the National Vaccine Injury Compensation Program, a national no-fault, nontort compensation scheme for people injured by compulsory childhood immunizations (see Pace and Dixon, 2017, and Neraas, 1988).[1] The program provides compensation for injuries attributed to diphtheria toxoid, tetanus toxoid, pertussis vaccine, measles vaccine, mumps vaccine, rubella vaccine, the polio vaccines, and combinations thereof (Ridgway, 1999). Under the act, prior to filing a civil action in court, an injured person must fully adjudicate the claim or claims through the program (42 U.S.C. § 300aa-11[a][2][A]). This adjudication process entails the following steps:

1. The claimant files a petition with the U.S. Court of Federal Claims. The petition includes an affidavit and documentation demonstrating that the injured person received a qualifying vaccine (that is, one listed in the act's vaccine injury table).
2. If the petitioner demonstrates, by a preponderance of the evidence, that the injured person received a vaccine included in the vaccine injury table, compensation is awarded (Neraas, 1988). This decision is made by a special master (Ridgway, 1999).

---

[1]   This compensation scheme was aimed at protecting the national vaccine supply. Prior to the passage of the act, an increasing number of vaccine injury lawsuits led to market instability and vaccine shortages (Neraas, 1988, p. 156).

In general, scholars have favorably evaluated the program's impact. Just two years after its passage, the act was characterized as "a superior vaccine injury compensation program to the tort recovery system" (Neraas, 1988, p. 158). The act was a "necessary alternative" to a tort system that was "unworkable" because of the "courts' inconsistent and unpredictable application of the duty to warn standard to vaccine manufacturers" and provided a "fair compensation scheme" to injured parties (Neraas, 1988, p. 158). Other scholars have considered the act's applicability beyond the world of vaccines. One scholar has characterized the act's compensation scheme as a "model of no-fault insurance" (Ridgway, 1988, p. 83).[2]

The Price–Anderson Act
A national no-fault insurance system has also been enacted in the nuclear power industry. In 1957, the U.S. Congress passed the Price–Anderson Act (Pub. L. No. 85-256, as codified at 42 U.S.C. § 2210).[3] The Price–Anderson Act was intended to promote investment in nuclear energy research by imposing statutory constraints on possible catastrophic tort liability in the event of a nuclear accident (Rabin, 1993). Scholars have criticized the Price–Anderson Act, however, arguing that it does not properly incentivize operators of nuclear reactors (Rabin, 1993).

National No-Fault Insurance for Autonomous Vehicle Technologies
Despite the examples discussed above, the stakeholders interviewed questioned whether the introduction of a national no-fault insurance system for the AV industry was warranted as a matter of policy. They noted that the risks associated with the AV industry, as well as the economics of the industry, are very different from those associated with either the vaccine industry or the nuclear industry. AVs, even though they may gain popularity, are much less prevalent than vaccines. An AV is also probably safer than a nuclear power plant. Although vaccines have caused relatively uniform injuries across incidents, one stakeholder noted, there is likely to be more variability in the harms caused by AVs. One interviewee from a manufacturer of AVs questioned whether vehicle autonomy represented a key national interest to the same degree as vaccines. As explained earlier, national no-fault auto insurance for AVs, if it were mod-

---

[2]   However, at least one expert has characterized the act, and experiences of navigating the Vaccine Injury Compensation Program, as "fall[ing] far short of expectations" because it lacks both consistency and speed in resolving claims. See, e.g., Engstrom, 2015, p. 1677.

[3]   The act has no formal title but has come to be known as the Price–Anderson Nuclear Industries Indemnity Act, or the Price–Anderson Act for short.

eled on the National Childhood Vaccine Injury Act, would require certain steps to adjudicate claims.[4]

A large majority of stakeholders opposed the introduction of a national no-fault insurance model. Many emphasized that a national no-fault insurance system would "create perverse incentives" for manufacturers and act as a "shield for irresponsible vehicle developers." One stakeholder predicted that such a system would "take away the incentive" for manufacturers "to do the best possible job."[5] If liability were apportioned regardless of fault, the economic incentives created by the tort system to increase safety would be substantially diluted.[6]

Even those stakeholders who did not oppose the adoption of a national no-fault insurance system thought that it was unlikely to happen. One manufacturer noted that, because such a scheme would require congressional action, it probably would not be successful. Another stakeholder told us that, even if a national no-fault insurance statute were somehow enacted, the federal bureaucracy was not equipped to administer a complex statutory insurance program. One insurer characterized a national no-fault insurance system as an interesting, but ultimately premature, idea that might make

---

[4] Under the act, prior to filing a civil action in court, an injured party must fully adjudicate the claims through the program (42 U.S.C. § 300aa-11[a][2][A]). As noted earlier, this adjudication process entails the following steps:

1. The claimant files a petition with the U.S. Court of Federal Claims. The petition includes an affidavit and documentation demonstrating that the injured person received a qualifying vaccine (one in the act's vaccine injury table).
2. If the petitioner demonstrates, by a preponderance of the evidence, that the injured person received a vaccine included in the vaccine injury table, compensation is awarded (Neraas, 1988). This decision is made by a special master (Ridgway, 1999).

[5] Legal scholars agree that manufacturers should bear some degree of responsibility for injuries arising out of the operation of AVs. For example, Kenneth S. Abraham and Robert L. Rabin have proposed what they term *manufacturer enterprise responsibility* (MER) (Abraham and Rabin, 2019, p. 5). To avoid inconsistency among state liability regimes, Abraham and Rabin conceived of MER as a single national rule enacted by Congress. MER would provide compensation to occupants of AVs and to third parties for bodily injuries "arising out of the operation" of an AV (p. 5). Abraham and Rabin argued that allocating responsibility to manufacturers would incentivize manufacturers' investment in research aimed at accident avoidance (pp. 29–30). The manufacturer-responsibility approach has the added advantage of encouraging manufacturers to internalize the cost of accidents involving AVs. This would prevent an "excessive" number of AVs from taking over the road. As an alternative, Mark Geistfeld proposed a system in which a manufacturer would be relieved of future tort liability so long as premarket testing demonstrated that the AV in question performed at least twice as safely as a conventional vehicle (Geistfeld, 2017). "By testing the autonomous vehicle to the point at which it performs at least twice as safely as conventional vehicles," Geistfeld explains, "the manufacturer will conclusively show that the fully functioning operating system is reasonably safe and not defectively designed" (p. 1653).

[6] Suppose, for example, that manufacturer A's cars are safer than manufacturer B's cars. If the manufacturers are liable either via products liability or through subrogation, they may have significant incentives to improve safety. But under a no-fault system, that incentive would be significantly diluted because the manufacturers' liability would not be affected by changes in the safety of their vehicles.

sense in a fully autonomous world, noting that "we are a very long way away from [such a world] today."

A State No-Fault Insurance Model for Autonomous Vehicles

In the past, state no-fault auto insurance schemes have not lived up to expectations (Anderson, Heaton, and Carroll, 2010). State no-fault insurance is

> a type of automobile insurance in which claims for personal injury (and some-times property damage) are made against the claimant's own insurance company (no matter who was at fault) rather than against the insurer of the party at fault. Under such state "no-fault" statutes only in cases of serious personal injuries and high medical costs may the injured bring an action against the other party or his insurer. No-fault statutes vary from state to state in terms of scope of coverage, threshold amounts, etc. (Black, 1983, p. 412)[7]

Stakeholders noted that state-level no-fault insurance systems have reduced neither the number of claims nor the cost of insurance. The authors of a 2010 RAND study of state no-fault insurance concluded,

> There is some evidence that no-fault's advantages in reducing litigation have decreased over time. Indicators of fraudulent claiming have also risen in no-fault states from their levels in the early 1990s. Thus, no-fault seems to have grown more expensive over time. This has led to a decline in support. (Anderson, Heaton, and Carroll, 2010, p. 136)

Insurance experts advised us that premiums in states with no-fault insurance systems are generally higher than premiums in states with fault-based systems.[8] In addition, insurers underscored the perception that a state no-fault insurance model leads to "rampant fraud and abuse."[9] As one stakeholder told us, "No-fault [insurance] has never worked." Many people have a "visceral reaction to no-fault insurance," noted an

---

[7] See also Anderson, Heaton, and Carroll, 2010, pp. 11–17.

[8] According to, for example, Insurance Information Institute, undated,

> Fraud is driving up the cost of auto insurance for New York State drivers, particularly those who live in New York City's five boroughs and its neighboring suburbs. As a result, some people are paying four times more for no-fault auto insurance than the state average and seven times more than drivers in Albany, which has fewer cases of fraud.

[9] See, e.g., Gusman, 2006, p. 21:

> . . . [O]ne problem that has hit New York and New Jersey particularly hard has been fraud. This fraud has been perpetrated by criminals—some functioning in highly-organized "fraud rings"—who have found ways to exploit the no fault system for their own financial gain.

insurer, suggesting that the implementation of a state no-fault insurance scheme for AVs would be difficult. A major manufacturer reminded us, moreover, that each state has already decided whether to introduce a no-fault insurance system.

Stakeholders expressed concerns that a state no-fault insurance model would not properly incentivize manufacturers to design and produce safe AVs. It was noted that "costs make people act better." According to one expert, a state no-fault insurance model would "let manufacturers off the hook" if they put unsafe AVs on the road. Studies by the Insurance Institute for Highway Safety support the view that, if provided with the incentive to improve crashworthiness, auto manufacturers could make significant gains in providing safer vehicles.[10] As we discussed in Chapter Two, a manufacturer may control the speed and driving characteristics of the vehicle and the way it reacts to other vehicles and environmental hazards in a way to most efficiently balance safety with transportation efficiency. For this reason, the deterrence justification of tort law probably suggests increased liability on the part of those parties that are best able to control the automation, the vehicle design, and its integration, which are, most likely, the manufacturers.

At the same time, a sizable number of stakeholders responded positively to the idea of introducing a state no-fault insurance model for AVs. Manufacturer interviewees told us that a state no-fault insurance model was still "on the table," characterizing it as a "remarkably good idea" and a "handy way of looking at autonomy." Although state no-fault insurance systems have been criticized, many stakeholders remain optimistic about the future prospects of such systems. Because claims involving AVs will also involve understanding the interrelated functioning of many component parts, a state no-fault insurance model would, in theory, make it easier for a victim to recover payment. Rather than having to identify who was at fault in a complex causal chain leading to a crash, a victim could simply recover payment directly from his or her own insurer. Even those stakeholders who noted the potential benefits of a state no-fault insurance model, however, did not believe that it was a realistic option. "It would be

---

The Insurance Research Council (IRC) stated about Florida's no-fault insurance system,

> A new report from the Insurance Research Council (IRC) estimates that Florida's third party bad-faith legal environment added an average of $106 in claim costs to every insured vehicle in the state in 2017, and resulted in a total of $7.6 billion in additional claim costs over the past 12 years. (IRC, 2018)

See also IRC, 2014, p. 2:

> By 2013, BI (bodily injury) liability claim frequency in Florida, a no-fault state, was greater than in most tort-system states. A key objective with no-fault insurance is to limit access to BI liability coverage reimbursement and provide easy access to first-party no-fault reimbursement. As a result, BI claim frequency rates in no-fault states are generally quite low. But this is no longer the case in Florida.

[10] See Zuby, undated, pp. 1–2 ("Since 1995, IIHS [the Insurance Institute for Highway Safety] has created a rigorous program of crash test ratings that have led to measureable improvements in the crash protection offered by modern vehicles"). See also Teoh and Lund, 2011.

great to have a new insurance regime," one stakeholder commented, "but we have to work with what we have. We can't let the perfect become the enemy of the good."

Manufacturers of Autonomous Vehicles May Self-Insure and Offer Insurance Services for Consumers

Several stakeholders indicated that, instead of purchasing insurance policies, manufacturers might self-insure. *Self-insurance* can be defined as "the practice of setting aside a fund to meet losses instead of insuring against such through insurance. A common practice of businesses is to self-insure up to a certain amount, and then to cover any excess with insurance" (Black, 1983, p. 707). In fact, one start-up indicated that, because of its leadership's high level of confidence in the safety of the company's technology, they plan to self-insure their deployed fleets. One expert noted that, after the initial, experimental phase of deployment, manufacturers might be incentivized to self-insure.

Relatedly, manufacturers of AVs might also launch their own insurance products. In May 2019, for example, Tesla introduced its own insurance product for Tesla drivers (Howard, 2019). One expert predicted that, in the future, the cost of insurance would be bundled with the AV itself. "From the point of view of safety," he noted, this model "makes a lot of sense." In the future, the expert added, insurers will try to sell auto insurance coverage policies to car manufacturers and software manufacturers rather than to individual consumers. Car manufacturers might carry their own insurance for the AVs they produce. The rationale for this model is as follows, the expert explained: "If I [the manufacturer] want to have a competitive car that's autonomous, I want the insurance [to be] part of my enterprise."

However, as explained in Chapter Two, unless a manufacturer incorporates an existing insurance company, self-insurance would require a network of claim adjusters, relationships with body shops, arbitrators, and lawyers—a vast skilled workforce whose primary function is to resolve the enormous volume of minor crashes. Even if automation dramatically reduces the incidence of at-fault crashes by avoiding human error, there are likely to be many crashes that still involve human-driven vehicles that will need to be resolved (see "Automobile Tort Law in Practice" in Chapter Two). However, as we noted in Chapter Two, as the automation becomes a more important factor in predicting risk than human behavior is, the manufacturer may be better positioned to collect the information necessary to underwrite efficiently. Even if humans are driving, manufacturers may be able to more easily collect rich data on human driving behavior and the sources of risk than insurers. Manufacturers, however, lack experience in navigating the state-based insurance regulatory system with 50 different legal regimes. This could be a significant impediment to offering competing insurance products (see "Conclusion" in Chapter Two).

Fleet Insurance Policies

In our discussions with stakeholders, we explored whether new business models for the deployment of AVs might have an effect on automobile insurance. The majority of experts cited fleets as the most likely model for the future deployment of AVs.[11] In insurance, *fleet policy* means a "blanket policy which covers a number of vehicles owned by the same insured; e.g., covers pool or fleet of vehicles owned by business" (Black, 1983, p. 410). One insurance expert suggested that, in the future, there may be multiple parties involved in AV fleets: an OEM, which would sell or lease AVs to a large company, such as a national grocery chain or a ride-hailing company (e.g., Uber), and a maintenance company that would provide routine care, repair, and housing for the AVs on a decentralized basis. This arrangement might raise insurance liability questions for fleet operations. Fleets, one insurer emphasized, are "where we are headed." According to one manufacturer, the "only opportunity for [autonomous] vehicles to be on the road" in the next five to ten years is "in a fleet circumstance." The cost of purchasing and maintaining an AV will make personal ownership prohibitive, stakeholders repeatedly noted, making a fleet model a more realistic possibility. Several stakeholders indicated that fleets would become dominant once AVs reach Level 4.[12]

The deployment of AVs in fleets is not a new phenomenon. As several stakeholders noted, AVs are already deployed in limited circumstances, including shuttle services and people movers in airports. Insurer interviewees expressed confidence that the deployment of fleets of AVs would not represent a significant challenge to the insurance industry. The insurance industry, we were told, would handle AV fleets "the way they always have." That is, the owners of fleets will choose to self-insure or to purchase insurance under corporate general liability policies. One manufacturer interviewee told us that the company already insures its fleets of nonautonomous vehicles under corporate general liability policies. Existing fleet insurance policies for limousines and taxis provide another model for insuring fleets of AVs in the future. The transition to fleets of AVs will likely be modeled on this existing approach to insurance. Stakeholders indicated that, under this model, fleet owners should bear responsibility for accidents caused by AVs.[13] As we explained in Chapter Two, owners of fleets of AVs may be in

---

[11] Although many experts predicted that the fleet model would eventually become dominant, in this chapter, we have focused much of our analysis on existing consumer insurance models. This approach was taken to test the applicability of consumer insurance models to claims involving AVs and to underscore that, even in a world in which fleets are dominant, it is likely that some consumers will continue to rely on privately owned and insured vehicles.

[12] One insurance expert noted, in a May 28, 2020, email to the authors, that existing transportation network company insurance laws may provide a template for fleet insurance policies.

[13] As we discussed in Chapter Two, under tort theory, in the example of a fleet operator with commercial insurance, the compensation rationale may suggest a retention of the operator rather than the manufacturer as being primarily responsible. In most cases, fleet operators are likely to have to comply with either Federal Motor Vehicle Carrier Administration requirements for liability insurance or analogous state provisions, and the required liabil-

a good position to contract with commercial insurers to provide adequate insurance. They may be large enough to develop sufficient internal expertise on handling claims or may contract with an insurer with this expertise. From an underwriting perspective, they may also have sufficient data to calculate appropriate risk premiums, particularly if the primary determinant of that premium is the vehicle rather than the driver (see the discussion in "Conclusion" in Chapter Two).

Although most stakeholders stated that the fleet model was likely to become dominant, one manufacturer interviewee cautioned that it is still too soon to develop "any concrete business model" for the deployment of AVs in fleets. In addition, stakeholders noted that it is important to think about the broader societal implications of relying on fleets. As one stakeholder put it, when someone rides in a fleet, that person "gives up rights."[14] Future research is needed to determine how fleets will affect the rights of individual riders.

Personal Mobility Policies

In addition to the models discussed already, one expert noted the possibility of listing the manufacturer of an AV as an additional insured on a personal insurance policy. Several experts raised the emerging concept of personal mobility policies. A personal mobility policy would allow someone who does not own a vehicle to protect themselves from liability associated with riding in fleets, using public transportation, and using shared mobility platforms. Experts told us, however, that the "market is not quite ready" for personal mobility policies yet. They also raised potential ethical issues associated with personal mobility policies, including that such policies "make the victim responsible for protecting against [the] negligence" of others—although it could be argued that this is the function of conventional automobile insurance policies as well. However, not all of the experts we interviewed believed that personal mobility policies would catch on. One expert responded that personal mobility policies "sound[ed] like an invention of someone [who] is afraid of losing individual clients." The expert characterized personal mobility policies as "absurd," noting that insurance companies were "trying to find a way to keep individuals [as customers] because they have agents to think about and they're thinking about what happens when the car insurance industry disappears." The expert added, "I wouldn't buy that. If I'm hurt on Metro, I'll sue Metro because that's Metro's problem."

---

ity insurance is relatively large and far more likely to cover injuries. To the extent that fleets can operate without such liability insurance, the compensation rationale would suggest shifting liability to the manufacturers. See the discussion in "Deterrence" in Chapter Two.

[14] For example, a mandatory arbitration clause may be applicable.

Adaptation of the Existing Automobile Insurance Framework

Several stakeholders we interviewed observed that, as automotive technology has evolved in the past century, the insurance industry has proven to be a remarkably resilient institution. In recognition of this resilience, many stakeholders, representing both manufacturers and the insurance industry, expressed optimism that the existing insurance framework would be able to adapt to the deployment of AVs (see Travelers Institute, 2018, p. 5). As one manufacturer interviewee told us, there is "no reason that the current system cannot keep working." Experts noted the historical resilience of the insurance industry in the face of persistent technological innovation. For example, the auto insurance industry has taken steps in the past few years to harness technology to identify and reduce fraud, especially in auto insurance claims. The Coalition Against Insurance Fraud reported,

> In the last two years, the technology offerings in the anti-fraud space have increased as new players have entered the field. Sources of data, especially from public sources, have grown as well. With increased competition and more outsourced services, costs in some areas have declined. This has allowed more insurers to expand their scope of tools to detect and investigate fraud. Smaller insurers especially have jumped onboard the anti-fraud technology train. (Coalition Against Insurance Fraud, 2019, p. 12)

In the future, as in the past, the "usual wheels of business will turn, and the professionals will figure it out," as one expert told us. Another expert underscored that the existing insurance framework "does not need to be blown up and replaced with something new." Rather, the "existing structure [of the insurance industry] can and will adapt to the different needs of higher levels of automation."

At the same time, some experts suggested that the existing automobile insurance system in the United States would not be able to adapt to AVs. When asked whether current automobile insurance models would exist in the future, one expert from the insurance industry stated, "Definitely not. I don't think [that the models] will stay the same at all." This expert continued, "A lot of the insurance will be manufacturer's insurance. If the car makes an error, it will be a manufacturer error." The expert concluded, "Ultimately, when the car will be driving autonomously, the liability will have to shift away from the driver [and] the cost of insurance will be bundled with the vehicle."

Even those stakeholders who anticipated changes in the insurance industry thought that the status quo would persist for the foreseeable future. Those insurer interviewees who foresaw changes in the industry were split as to whether those changes would occur at Level 3 or 4. One insurance industry expert observed, "It's going to be a sloppy transition; it's not going to happen all at once." The expert added, "I think the bulk of it will happen when we move to [Levels] 4 and 5." (Table 3.3 shows interview-

Table 3.3
At Which Level of Autonomy Will Changes to the Existing U.S. Insurance Framework Become Necessary?

When Change Would Be Necessary	Responses
At Level 3	1
At Level 4	3
Unsure, but changes will be necessary at some point	5
The existing insurance framework will adapt; changes will not be significant in the foreseeable future.	17

NOTE: We have included only U.S. stakeholders. Each response reflects one interview. Some interviews included multiple participants.

ees' additional thoughts on this subject.) One manufacturer interviewee noted that, because the transition would be gradual rather than an abrupt shift, it would be unwise to make immediate changes to the existing insurance framework. Several stakeholders cautioned against "solv[ing] everything too far in advance," noting that it would be prudent to wait to gather more information about the losses associated with AVs. "We should wait until we know what the facts are before we talk about adjusting the business and regulatory models. Until we actually see the facts on the ground and whether adjustment is required," one stakeholder told us, it would be too soon to make radical changes. "It may be," the stakeholder reminded us, that the "existing models have the flexibility required to handle [autonomous] vehicles."

Autonomous Vehicles in Auto Insurance Claim Scenarios

We asked stakeholders about specific types of insurance claim incidents that might occur with AVs and how they would be handled. These incidents were

- an AV colliding with a conventional vehicle
- an accident involving an AV and a pedestrian
- property damage to an AV (such as that caused by hail or a tree limb).

As described in this section, stakeholders indicated that the existing auto insurance framework would be able to adapt to AVs in each instance.

A Crash Involving an Autonomous Vehicle and a Conventional Car

We asked stakeholders about how common insurance scenarios might be handled when an AV was added to the scenario. We inquired whether the claims process would need to change significantly. A majority of stakeholders indicated that, for accidents involving AVs and conventional cars, the claims process would not change significantly. As one expert explained, accidents "will be handled like we handle accidents today." For an accident involving severe injuries, however, the injured party might consider suing the AV manufacturer if the losses exceeded the policy limit of the AV driver or owner. Even for more-minor accidents, the insurer of the vehicle driver or owner might pursue a subrogation claim against the insurer of the conventional vehicle. These actions would entail significant changes to cost incidence, even if much of the process of making and adjudicating an insurance claim looked the same.

We also asked experts whether the subrogation process was likely to change for future auto insurance models. Subrogation is "the lawful substitution of a third party in place of a party having a claim against another party." Specifically, "[i]nsurance companies . . . generally have the right to step into the shoes of the party whom they compensate and sue any party whom the compensated party could have sued" (Black, 1983, p. 743). Most stakeholders indicated that the deployment of AVs would not affect subrogation. Subrogation is a "big part of what [insurers] do" today, and insurer interviewees told us that they would continue to handle the subrogation process in the same way. As one insurer interviewee told us, "We'll pursue our subrogation—you can be assured of that." In particular, insurer interviewees explained that they often pursued subrogation against suppliers of component parts. Although the deployment of AVs may create a more complex ecosystem of suppliers and, in some cases, make determining which supplier was at fault more difficult, insurer interviewees anticipated continuing to "handle this like [they] handle suppliers today." One stakeholder noted, however, that insurers would be less concerned about being able to pursue subrogation against manufacturers that handle all or most hardware and software in-house. The different business models of AV manufacturers will affect the extent to which subrogation remains a common feature of the claims process.[15]

A Crash Involving an Autonomous Vehicle and a Pedestrian

In response to our questions about how common automobile insurance scenarios might be handled if an AV were involved, many stakeholders indicated that accidents between AVs and pedestrians would be handled the same way as those between conventional cars and pedestrians. In contrast to the claims process, however, for an accident involving severe injuries, the injured party might consider suing the AV manufacturer if the losses exceeded the policy limit of the AV driver or owner.[16] Pedestrians care less about the kind of vehicle that harms them than about being compensated for that harm. As one manufacturer told us, "If I'm a pedestrian and you run me over, I sue under your

---

[15] One insurance expert noted in a May 28, 2020, email to the authors that subrogation serves an important deterrent purpose by creating appropriate incentives for OEMs and part suppliers to take steps to prevent the use of defective products.

[16] Comment of insurance expert, March 26, 2020.

primary auto policy. If I'm struck by an autonomous vehicle, I sue under the policy of the owner or registrant." Other stakeholders predicted that the severity of accidents involving pedestrians would go down because AVs "won't be speeding and will brake" for pedestrians. At the same time, new issues are likely to emerge. Pedestrians are inherently unpredictable, and the technologies embedded in AVs will need to be able to "anticipate the unexpected" on busy city streets.

Property Damage to an Autonomous Vehicle

We asked the stakeholders we interviewed about property damage, a common claim under current conventional automobile insurance policies, and whether handling of claims might change in the future. Many stakeholders indicated that insurance for property damage would not change for AVs. The majority of the experts we interviewed stated that increasing levels of autonomy do not necessarily increase the risk of property damage. The claims process would not change, stakeholders noted, although it may be more expensive. Specifically, one manufacturer told us, it "seems hard to see a reason to change" how property damage claims are currently handled. "The fact that it's a more expensive vehicle to insure shouldn't affect the procedure." At the end of the day, an insurer explained, "if the car is on fire, it's the same [process] whether or not it's autonomous." One expert noted that people are often shocked by the cost of repairing new cars when their expensive sensors have been damaged and indicated that the cost of repairing sensors in AVs may result in higher insurance rates. "These claims won't be different—they'll just cost more." One stakeholder concluded, "The risks of property damage are the same for AVs and non-AVs."

At the same time, new concerns about property damage are likely to emerge as AVs become more popular. Some stakeholders told us that, in the absence of a human driver, the physical security of AVs may be at risk. One start-up interviewee, however, questioned this view, asserting that property damage would become a thing of the past because most AVs would be operated as fleets and stored in secure locations.

Conclusion

The different models that have been discussed in this chapter can be summarized according to several criteria that have been identified by the experts we interviewed:

- whether legislative action would be required
- potential incentive or disincentive for manufacturer safety improvements
- fraud concerns
- ease of the claims process
- application to all levels of automation.

A national no-fault system would require legislative action, create a potential disincentive for manufacturer safety improvements, require a bureaucratic governmental claims process, and apply only to AVs that operate at Level 4 or 5, depending on how the enacting legislation defined *autonomy*.

Expansion of the current state no-fault automobile insurance model would require state legislative action, could create a potential disincentive for manufacturer safety improvements, and might promote fraud concerns, according to the experts we interviewed. However, it might have an easy claims process and apply to all levels of automation.

Manufacturer self-insurance might promote an incentive for manufacturer safety improvements. This model would not require legislative action. However, the ease of claims processing and potential for fraud are unknown. This model would apply to vehicles that operate at Levels 4 and 5.

Fleet insurance policies would not require legislative action, could provide an incentive for manufacturers to improve safety, and would have a well-established claims process. Fleet insurance policies may apply to all levels of automation.

Existing automobile insurance models would not require legislative action, would provide incentives for manufacturers to improve safety, would have a well-known claims process, and would apply to all levels of automation. U.S. automobile insurance companies have taken action to combat fraud in auto insurance claims (see, e.g., Coalition Against Insurance Fraud, 2019, p. 12).

Perhaps the most important feature of an insurance framework for AVs is how effectively it would compensate the victims of accidents. In the UK, Australia, Canada, and Japan, swift compensation for victims of auto accidents is a stated regulatory goal for new auto insurance frameworks that include AVs. In Chapter Four, we explore these new international auto insurance frameworks.

International Models for Insuring Autonomous Vehicles

This chapter provides an overview of recent developments in insurance and the regulation of AVs in the UK, Australia, Canada, and Japan. We selected these countries because compensating the injured is a guiding principle of their auto insurance frameworks. In addition to reviewing legislation, draft regulations, white papers, and other materials, we interviewed regulatory and insurance experts from all four countries. The focus of this inquiry was how other countries were adapting their insurance models to accommodate AVs.

In the UK, the Automated and Electric Vehicles Act 2018 (AEVA) became law on July 19, 2018. AEVA is applicable across the UK, with the exception of sections 1 through 8, which cover insurance for AVs and apply only to Great Britain (Butcher and Edmonds, 2018). A parliamentary briefing paper explained,

> [T]he intention behind the legislation is to emphasise that if there is an insurance "event" (accident) the compensation route for the individual remains with the motor insurance settlement framework, rather than through a product liability framework against a manufacturer. (Butcher and Edmonds, 2018, p. 3)

The UK's motor insurance settlement framework serves as an insurer of last resort, so that anyone injured in an auto accident is provided with full insurance coverage and access to compensation.

Australia is of particular interest for the United States, because auto insurance there operates at a state level like it does in the United States, so some states have no-fault auto insurance schemes and others do not. In some states, auto insurance is provided by private insurers; in others, it is provided by the government. Australia also has a National Injury Insurance Scheme (NIIS), which ensures that "people who sustain eligible serious or catastrophic, lifetime injuries in motor vehicle accidents (regardless of fault) receive necessary and reasonable treatment, care and support" (National Transport Commission [NTC], 2018, p. 16). In addition, each Australian state and territory has laws that require every registered vehicle to have motor accident injury insurance (MAII). Currently, regulators are in the process of consulting with the insurance industry and the public to determine how to modify MAII to cover injuries caused by automated vehicles and AVs.

The Insurance Bureau of Canada (IBC), a trade association with membership representing 90 percent of the Canadian insurance market, has recommended "[a] single insurance policy that covers both driver negligence and the automated technology" that "would ensure that vehicles continue to be properly insured and that people injured in collisions involving automated vehicles are compensated fairly and quickly" (IBC, 2018, p. 11). IBC has explained that "[t]he single insurance policy's intent is to align the tort process for automated vehicle claims with traditional claims involving conventional vehicles" (IBC, 2018, p. 11). Of particular interest to insurance regulators in the United States is that the single insurance policy proposed by IBC "can co-exist with the mixed no-fault and tort policies that are common in Canada" (IBC, 2018, p. 10). As of this writing, IBC's proposal for a single insurance policy has not been adopted.

Japan has a mandatory auto insurance system that is focused on providing full compensation to victims of accidents. Every driver has to obtain insurance. The owner of a vehicle pays the premium, and, in the case of an accident, the victim is fully covered. According to our Japanese regulatory expert, the mandatory auto insurance system in Japan will be applied to AVs. Our expert explained that the Japanese approach is almost a national no-fault insurance system. Our expert thought that the Japanese auto insurance system would be workable up to and including Level 3 automation but that change would be necessary at Levels 4 and 5. Our expert suggested that, when most vehicles operate at Levels 4 and 5, AV manufacturers might pay the insurance premium that is currently paid by individual drivers and owners. Additional material about how all four of these countries are adapting their insurance models to accommodate AVs is provided in Appendix A.

The UK Model for Insuring Automated Vehicles Focuses on Quick and Easy Compensation for Victims

> **Key Ideas**
> UK regulators want victims of accidents to have quick and easy compensation. The UK insurance framework for automated vehicles, which was adopted through the legislative process, differs from that for U.S. auto insurance in that, even when there is no fault or the responsible driver cannot be identified, victims are assured of compensation. The existing UK framework that includes automated vehicles is intended to work through Level 3 of automation; for Levels 4 and 5, a new framework may be necessary. A novel feature of the new legislation is that, for vehicles operating at Levels 4 and 5, there will be compensation for the person in the driver's seat. A UK expert explained, "It adds an extra class of person that will be covered under the policy, because the person in the driver's seat becomes a victim when the AV takes over."

Currently, all vehicles on UK roads have to be insured in compliance with Section 143 of the Road Traffic Act 1988, as amended (UK Public General Acts, 1988 Ch. 52). Specifically, Section 145(3)(a) of the act requires that third-party risks be covered. Like the U.S. insurance framework, the UK's existing insurance framework provides that "in many cases of claims there is a determination of 'fault' and it will be the insurer of the 'at fault' driver which will pay the bulk of the claim" (Butcher and Edmonds, 2018, p. 5). However, unlike in the U.S. insurance structure, in the UK framework, "even where there is no 'fault,' victims are assured of compensation" (Butcher and Edmonds, 2018, p. 5). A parliamentary briefing paper explains that, "in cases where there is no insurance, or the other driver cannot be contacted, the Motor Insurers Bureau (MIB) steps in as insurer of last resort" (Butcher and Edmonds, 2018, p. 5). The paper concludes, "in short, the compensation process is driver-centric" (Butcher and Edmonds, 2018, p. 5). A UK regulatory expert explained, "if you lived in the UK and bought car insurance, you are not insuring your car. You're insuring against your negligence." He added that this "allows victims to have quick and easy compensation. We see that as being fine up to and including Level 3, because there is still a driver involved." He continued, "Broadly speaking, everyone agreed that the divide is between Level 3, where the current framework works, and Levels 4 and 5, where we need a new framework." The outcome UK regulators want, he said, "is for the victim to have quick and easy compensation, and the question is how to do this." He added that UK stakeholders and regulators had worked out "the minimum viable product for insurance." He stated, "[T]his policy position was tested with industry and the public, and there was broad support because it is relatively easy—although it took two and a half years to get that fix agreed to in Parliament."

The parliamentary "fix" that the UK expert mentioned is AEVA, which became law on July 19, 2018. AEVA is applicable across the UK, with the exception of sections 1 to 8, which cover insurance for AVs and extend only to Great Britain (Butcher and Edmonds, 2018). A parliamentary briefing paper explained,

> [T]he intention behind the legislation is to emphasise that if there is an insurance "event" (accident) the compensation route for the individual remains with the motor insurance settlement framework, rather than through a product liability framework against a manufacturer. (Butcher and Edmonds, 2018, p. 3)

An expert in the UK noted, "In the UK, we're obsessed with making sure that anyone who is involved in a road accident is fully protected." As for AEVA, he explained, it "says that if a vehicle is on the road, it needs to have [a Road Traffic Act 1988]–compliant motor traffic insurance policy in place." Furthermore, he stated, "[T]his is important because it provides unlimited coverage." Some key differences from the current U.S. insurance model are that, if there is a human with fallback capability (that is, who could take over the driving task), that human is responsible for an accident. So, for Level 2 automation, the responsibility for accidents lies with the driver. However, at Levels 4 and 5, if the vehicle is driving itself at the time and the person in the driver's seat is not in the fallback position, the person is not responsible for the accident. A UK insurance expert explained,

> [I]n the UK, if you are driving like an idiot and drive into a wall, you don't get any damages. When we get to Levels 4 and 5, there will be compensation for the person in the driver's seat. It adds an extra class of person that will be covered under the policy, because the person in the driver's seat becomes a victim when the AV takes over.

The new law also provides that the UK Secretary of State must prepare and keep up to date a list of all motor vehicles that

> (a) [a]re in the Secretary of State's opinion designed or adapted to be capable, in at least some circumstances or situations, of safely driving themselves and (b) [m]ay lawfully be used when driving themselves, in at least some circumstances or situations, on roads or other public places in Great Britain. (AEVA, 2018, p. 9)

A UK insurance expert commented on the development of the list of automated vehicles, "[T]he Law Commission is talking about a safety committee or an approval committee that would look at vehicles and make a recommendation to the Secretary of State. A vehicle would be submitted and then rubber-stamped by the safety committee." The UK insurance expert added, "We're looking at having a database that links from the VIN [vehicle identification number] to what features are available on the car.

I think manufacturers will see that, if they provide this information, it will be to their benefit."

The UK is also moving ahead with AV data-sharing initiatives. The UK insurance expert told us that there are conversations about the ownership, use, and control of AV data across Europe. He explained that there was a proposal to have a network of neutral servers, so data would go from the vehicle to the manufacturer, from the manufacturer to the neutral server, and from the neutral server to the insurer. The UK Department of Transport has been handling these discussions in Brussels. He noted that "the plan is to involve a U.S. element, but I haven't seen that yet."

The UK experts with whom we spoke indicated that they expected fleet ownership to precede private ownership of AVs, an expectation consistent with that of the U.S. experts we interviewed. A UK expert stated, "[O]ur view is that, while everyone is paying attention to private cars, we fully expect to see autonomous fleets ahead of widespread adoption of that technology in private cars."

Australia Examines Six Options to Cover People Injured in Crashes Involving Automated and Autonomous Vehicles

Key Ideas

NTC is leading efforts to make changes to Australia's MAII program to encompass automated vehicles. After extensive consultations with the insurance industry and the public, NTC will bring the recommendations to the Australian legislature. The focus of NTC's consultations is changes to MAII to provide for injuries that result from an accident involving an automated vehicle or AV. Each Australian state and territory has laws that require every registered vehicle to have MAII. The majority of comments received by NTC were that a consistent, national approach should be taken to provide cover for any injury that results from an automated driving system (ADS) crash, with "[t]he majority of stakeholders support[ing] expanding existing MAII schemes to cover injuries caused by an ADS" (NTC, 2019, p. 30). According to NTC,

> In the short to medium term cover for injuries should be provided by MAII schemes. The approach should be reviewed by MAII schemes when automated vehicles are a statistically sufficient portion of registered vehicles to enable assessment of their safety risks. (NTC, 2019, p. 30)

Earlier, in October 2018, NTC released a discussion paper, *Motor Accident Injury Insurance and Automated Vehicles*, for public comment. In the paper, NTC "identifies elements within existing motor accident injury insurance schemes that may act as barriers to accessing compensation for personal injuries or death caused by an automated driving system" (NTC, 2018, p. ii). The paper describes "how these schemes, or alternative insurance models, could provide cover for injuries and deaths involving an automated vehicle" (NTC, 2018, p. ii). Currently, NTC is analyzing the comments filed in response to the discussion paper.

Australia has a variety of different insurance schemes because of its federal/state system, which is similar to the U.S. system. Insurance schemes operate at the state level, with coverage that varies. An Australian regulatory expert explained that some states have full no-fault coverage, while others have different definitions that require a driver to be identified in a crash. In such a case, a crash caused by an AV would not be covered because a driver could not be identified. Some states require finding fault, which might be complicated for AVs. The current compulsory third-party insurance scheme is comparable to products liability in the United States. According to our Australian regulatory expert, state governments have been requiring products liability insurance to be in place. State regulators recognize that, "if you rely on products liability, you might have to go through a lengthy court battle to get compensation." For this reason, state regulators have recognized that there is a power imbalance between the manufacturer or developer and the person who is injured. The Australian expert explained that products liability is extensively used in Australia, but not in the road transport area, because Australia has a compulsory third-party insurance scheme. Australian courts use tests similar to those in the United States in products liability cases.

Australia also has the NIIS, which ensures that "people who sustain eligible serious or catastrophic, lifetime injuries in motor vehicle accidents (regardless of fault) receive necessary and reasonable treatment, care and support" (NTC, 2018, p. 16). According to the NTC discussion paper, "[a]ll states and territories [in Australia] have introduced laws . . . or amended existing laws . . . to implement the scheme" (NTC, 2018, p. 16). An Australian regulatory expert told us that NIIS works slightly differently in different states but that, essentially, it is attached to vehicle registration. For example, he said, "[I]n Victoria, it's paid as part of annual vehicle registration. In other states, where it's privately run, you buy it from an insurer and then provide proof when you register your car." The expert said that each state was able to implement NIIS in its own way, to establish a minimum level of coverage around the country. He commented that some states supported a similar approach for AV insurance because they like having the flexibility and it gives the public assurance of minimum coverage. However, he noted that the insurance industry is seeking a more national approach to AV insurance.

The NTC discussion paper states that "[l]aws in each Australian state and territory require every registered vehicle to have motor accident injury insurance (MAII)"

(NTC, 2018, p. 1). The authors of the discussion paper identified the following problems that stem from current MAII schemes:

> People injured or killed in an ADS crash may not have the same, or any, access to compensation under existing MAII schemes compared with those injured or killed in a crash involving a motor vehicle controlled at the time by a human driver.
>
> Current MAII laws do not contemplate an ADS "driving" a motor vehicle. MAII laws contain definitions that do not provide for an ADS being "in control of", being a "driver" of or "driving" a vehicle. One of the circumstances in which an injury or accident is eligible under these schemes is if it was caused by "the driving of" the vehicle. An ADS crash may not meet that requirement and access to compensation or benefits may be more restricted for those injured in an ADS crash.
>
> Many MAII schemes require fault to be proved for compensation to be paid. To obtain compensation under fault-based MAII schemes (and hybrid MAII schemes in limited circumstances), an injured party—for example, the driver or registered operator must be at fault. Even if an ADS were considered to be driving, it is not a person. An ADS is a machine and cannot be negligent. The entity responsible is not clear.
>
> Current MAII schemes are generally designed to cover injuries caused by human error rather than product faults. If MAII schemes were to cover ADS crash injuries, significant redesign of MAII schemes may be required to ensure that the cost of ADS crashes is borne by those who can control the risks. These parties may include manufacturers, automated driving system entities (ADSEs), communications providers and infrastructure owners rather than governments, insurers and vehicle owners. (NTC, 2018, pp. 1–2)

The NTC discussion paper outlines six options to address these problems. The first three options are based on current MAII arrangements, while the last three options would require new approaches. Further details about each option may be found in Appendix A. The six options are as follows:

- option 1: Rely on the existing legal framework.
- option 2: Exclude from MAII schemes any injury caused by an ADS.
- option 3: Expand MAII schemes to cover injuries caused by ADSs.
- option 4: Implement a purpose-built automated vehicle scheme.
- option 5: Set minimum benchmarks.
- option 6: Use a single insurer.

An Australian expert explained that Australian regulators recognize that what they develop needs to be proportional and scalable over time. The expert further stated that part of the regulators' rationale is the importance of using existing agencies and schemes. He commented, "If you tie it into existing schemes, it might give people more assurance." The expert noted that there appears to be some support from Australian states and the insurance industry, as well as regulators, for option 3 and that the next challenge regulators face will be pricing that option. The expert raised concerns about how to deal with vehicles that move between modes (i.e., autonomous to human-controlled) and questioned whether this might necessitate switching between different insurance schemes, which would be very challenging. The expert further indicated that, although option 3 is favored, regulators have also considered option 6, a single-insurer model that offers bundling, which is based on the model in the UK. The expert noted, "Everyone seems to like the UK model—there's an assumption that the AV is liable. A lot of our stakeholders like that model."

Another Australian expert noted that, "at a high level, Australia's transport ministers support using the existing motor accident insurance framework to support AVs." She added, "however, any changes to Australia's insurance framework requires the agreement of Treasurers. The matter is currently being considered by Treasurers, so the policy on AV insurance is not settled."[1]

Canadian Insurers Propose a Framework for Insuring Autonomous Vehicles That Covers Driver Negligence, Technology for Autonomous Vehicles, and Data-Sharing

> **Key Ideas**
> IBC has proposed a single insurance policy that covers both driver negligence and automated technology. The policy "would ensure that vehicles continue to be properly insured and that people injured in collisions involving automated vehicles are compensated fairly and quickly" (IBC, 2018, p. 11). IBC has noted that, "[u]nlike no-fault insurance, the single insurance policy can co-exist with the mixed no-fault and tort policies that are common in Canada" (IBC, 2018, p. 10). The IBC proposals have sparked interest but have not been implemented via legislation.

---

[1]   Correspondence with Australian regulatory expert, October 19, 2020. According to this expert, "In Australia, Ministerial responsibility for most of the MAII schemes sits (at least in part) with Treasurers. Treasurers are ministers with responsibility for government revenue and expenditure" (correspondence with the Australian regulatory expert, November 22, 2020).

For a 2018 publication, *Auto Insurance for Automated Vehicles: Preparing for the Future of Mobility*, IBC analysts evaluated three insurance models to address how the Canadian auto insurance industry might adapt to the introduction of AVs (IBC, 2018):

- Maintain the status quo.
- Establish full (national) no-fault insurance.
- Cover both driver negligence and the automated technology under a single insurance policy (IBC, 2018).

The authors recommended "[a] single insurance policy that covers both driver negligence and the automated technology" that "would ensure that vehicles continue to be properly insured and that people injured in collisions involving automated vehicles are compensated fairly and quickly" (IBC, 2018, p. 11). IBC explained that "[t]he single insurance policy's intent is to align the tort process for automated vehicle claims with traditional claims involving conventional vehicles" (IBC, 2018, p. 11). In the IBC publication, the bureau noted that, "[u]nlike no-fault insurance, the single insurance policy can co-exist with the mixed no-fault and tort policies that are common in Canada" (IBC, 2018, p. 10). For details on the proposed IBC insurance models, please see Appendix A.

A Canadian insurance expert explained, "[W]e have fault-determination rules in a lot of provinces." He added, "fault-determination rules are used in Ontario, New Brunswick, Nova Scotia, and Prince Edward Island. Alberta and Newfoundland don't use them, and other provinces have public insurance." According to the expert, the reason Canada has fault-determination rules is for those provinces that have direct compensation for property damage—when there is a collision, for property damage, the driver is compensated by his or her own insurance company. The expert clarified, "[T]o the degree you're not at fault, you collect from your own insurance company. If you are 50 [percent] at fault, your insurance company covers 50 [percent] of damages." The expert concluded, "These rules are based on years of jurisprudence and how the courts assigned fault in cases."

The insurance expert indicated that, once AV technology was introduced, an injured party would have to prove that the other party caused the accident. He explained that the IBC approach would enable someone injured in an accident with an AV to say, "[T]hat vehicle hit me and caused the collision, rather than whether the technology played a role." He discussed the UK model as an important influence on the IBC recommendations. He stated that, under the UK model, "the auto insurance would pay out regardless of whether the person or the technology was at fault." He added, "[A]fter paying the claim, the insurance company could recover from the technology provider." However, he stated that Canadian auto insurers thought that there should be a deductible, which is not the case with the UK model. He commented, "You can't subrogate the entire claim. The insurance company should retain at least some of the liability loss associated with the technology malfunction, instead of just passing the cost onto the vehicle manufacturer." The expert concluded, "What's so great about the UK proposal is that it fits on top of the mixed no-fault and tort systems in Canada."

An important aspect of the IBC framework is a data-sharing arrangement between vehicle manufacturers and insurers. The IBC proposal states,

> The data-sharing arrangement would consist of vehicle manufacturers making prescribed data available to vehicle owners and/or insurers to help determine the cause of a collision, whether the vehicle was in manual or automated mode at the time of the collision and the vehicle operator's interaction with the automated technology. A data sharing arrangement is crucial to a quick resolution of liability claims. (IBC, 2018, p. 12)

The IBC report explains that the process for data-sharing should be streamlined and "avoid any administrative burden on vehicle manufacturers, vehicle owners or insurers," although how this might be accomplished is not described (IBC, 2018, p. 12). IBC's recommended data-sharing arrangement includes the following data elements:

- Global Positioning System (GPS)–event time stamp
- GPS-event location
- automated status (on or off)
- automated mode (parking or driving)
- automated transition time stamp
- record of driver intervention of steering or braking, throttle or indicator
- time since last driver interaction
- driver seat occupancy
- driver belt latch
- speed
- vehicle warnings or notifications to the vehicle's operator (IBC, 2018).

According to the IBC publication, "Thatcham Research, the U.K. insurance industry's vehicle safety and research centre, deems the first nine data elements necessary to support the single insurance policy prescribed in the Automated and Electric Vehicles Bill" (IBC, 2018, p. 13). The authors noted that the two other data elements provide relevant information from the vehicle's dashboard. The Canadian insurance expert we interviewed noted that IBC officials did not think that any of the data elements proposed contained proprietary information. The expert asked, "If a claim would proceed through litigation, this data would have to be made available anyway, so why not make it available earlier in the process?"

In Japan, the Current Mandatory Insurance System Applies to Automated Vehicles but May Need to Change

Key Ideas
Japan has a mandatory auto insurance system that is focused on providing full compensation to victims of accidents. Every driver has to obtain insurance. The owner of a vehicle pays the premium, and, in the case of an accident, the victim is fully covered. According to our Japanese regulatory expert, the mandatory auto insurance system in Japan will be applied to AVs. Changes to the Japanese automobile insurance system would be undertaken by the legislature.

We learned from a Japanese regulatory expert that Japan has a mandatory automobile insurance system, which requires every driver to obtain insurance. The owner of the car pays the premium or fee, and, in the event of an accident, the victim is covered. Everyone in Japan needs to pay for a specified level of insurance of at least ¥3 million. An ordinary driver can buy additional insurance for the car, for body damage, and for himself or herself. If there is an accident, the police come to investigate which vehicles' owners have responsibility or liability. Then, the insurance company pays the victims from the mandatory insurance. If the police discover that there was some negligence involved in the accident, there can be criminal penalties for the driver. The Japanese regulatory expert told us that the police do not make this determination. He explained, "It is very hard to escape liability for the accident in case of an injured person or fatality." According to the expert, the Japanese government has indicated that this mandatory insurance system would also be applied to AVs.

We learned that currently, a concrete definition of *automated vehicle* is being prepared in Japan. The Japanese House of Representatives and House of Councillors passed two important pieces of legislation on AVs in May 2019. The Road Transport Vehicle Act was revised on May 17, 2019, and the Road Traffic Act was amended on May 28, 2019. The expert indicated that the Japanese government intends to accelerate development of automated vehicles by enacting this legislation.

The Road Transport Vehicle Act (under the jurisdiction of the Ministry of Land, Infrastructure, Transport and Tourism [MLIT]) provides a detailed definition of the automated driving apparatus. In a November 9, 2020, email to the authors, the expert provided an unofficial but helpful translation of the provisions of the legislation:

> The "automatic operation device" is to process the sensor for detecting the operating state and surrounding conditions of the vehicle and the information transmitted from the sensor, which are necessary for the program to automatically operate the vehicle. This device whose main components are the computer and program of the above, and when each device is used under the conditions ordered by the Minister of Land, Infrastructure, Transport and Tourism, recognition, prediction, judgment and operation related to the operation of the person who operates the

automobile. This device that has a function to replace all of the capabilities related to the above and is equipped with a device for recording information necessary for confirming the operating state of the function.

The Road Traffic Act (under the jurisdiction of the National Police Agency) provides additional definition of *automated driving apparatus* and creates a requirement to record the necessary data to confirm the operating condition of the ADS. The expert provided the following unofficial translation of the act:

> (1) *The automated driving apparatus* means device [that is] defined by the Road Transport Vehicle Act and . . . (2) [The driver] shall not drive or make someone . . . drive an automated vehicle which could not properly record any necessary data to confirm [the] operating condition of [the] automated driving system. (3) [The user] of the vehicle [who] installed an automated driving apparatus shall keep the data recorded by the recording device in accordance with regulation [to] be decided by the Cabinet Office.

According to the expert, details about the exact data that must be recorded and how long those data should be stored will be specified in 2020. He advised us that MLIT is studying this subject carefully.

The new and amended legislation has a significant impact on how *automated vehicle* is defined in Japan. The expert characterized the change in a figure, replicated here as Figure 4.1.

When we asked the expert about the possible models for AV insurance in the future, he told us that the current system of insurance would be suitable for Levels 2 and 3, when the automated vehicle can request that the driver take over control of the vehicle and thus the risk of an accident. This means that premiums should be paid by the owner, and the owner could be liable for the accident. However, the expert suggested that, at Levels 4 and 5, "insurance . . . should be changed." He speculated that this change might be informed by products liability insurance. He suggested that, at Levels 4 and 5, the manufacturer of the AV would bear responsibility and, in this case, "the auto insurance premium should be paid by the manufacturer of the AV." Regarding other anticipated changes to the automobile insurance industry, the expert commented, "It is an important duty to modify or introduce a new insurance system, especially for AVs. Insurance could help or become an obstacle to every new development." He explained that AV insurance could be a kind of experiment for artificial intelligence (AI) devices in the near future. He agreed that AV insurance could serve as a prototype for other kinds of insurance in the future. The expert noted, "Everything related to AI will become more popular and big business, so AVs are a kind of experiment."

Figure 4.1
Japan's Definition of *Automated Vehicle*

Image prior to the legislation:

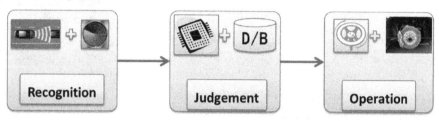

Definition by the legislation:

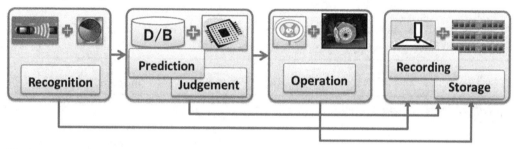

SOURCE: Masayuki Satoh, chief legal director, ITS Japan.

Similarities Exist in How the UK, Australia, Canada, and Japan Are Adapting Their Insurance Frameworks to Accommodate Autonomous Vehicles

Our research into how several countries are adapting—or proposing to adapt—their auto insurance frameworks to prepare for the introduction of AVs reveals some distinct similarities. Each of the countries has a focus on swift and easy compensation for accident victims. For this reason, a reliance on products liability litigation was not a primary or favored approach to compensating victims.[2] All of the countries we investigated followed an adaptive approach to incorporating AVs into auto insurance schemes. The experts we consulted indicated that the current framework for auto insurance would be flexible enough to accommodate automated vehicles up to Level 3 but that, once most vehicles were operating at Level 4 or Level 5 of automation, the auto insurance framework might need to change. Similarly, it appeared that, although countries were preparing to deal with the new challenges that might be posed by AVs, policymakers

---

[2]   It should be noted that each of these countries has a stronger social safety net than that in the United States, including more-widespread access to medical insurance, which might explain why they rely less on products liability litigation to make victims whole following an accident.

intended to assess developments in the technology before undertaking any major over-haul of the existing auto insurance framework. As one Australian expert noted, Australian regulators recognize that what they develop needs to be proportional and scalable over time. Other countries, such as the UK and Japan, are focused on having insurance coverage for all drivers. Policymakers in several countries, such as the UK, Japan, and Canada, are considering data-sharing arrangements between and among vehicle manufacturers, insurers, and other stakeholders. The Japanese expert observed that the framework for AV auto insurance could either help or delay the deployment of AVs, an important point for consideration by regulators and policymakers in the United States.

Table 4.1 illustrates some of the similarities and differences of the auto insurance frameworks we have discussed in this chapter.

Table 4.1

A Comparison of Frameworks in the UK, Australia, Canada, and Japan for Insuring Autonomous Vehicles

Characteristic	UK	Australia (proposed)	Canada (proposed)	Japan
Ubiquitous coverage of drivers and victims	Yes	Yes	Yes	For victims but not drivers
Minimum insurance coverage for all drivers	Yes	Yes	Yes	No
Mandatory	Yes	Yes	Yes	Yes
Full compensation for victims	Yes	Yes	Yes[a]	Limited
Applies to automated vehicles	Yes	Yes	Yes	Yes
National program	Yes	Yes	Unclear	Yes
Paid by insurance premium	Yes	Yes	Yes	Yes
Paid by vehicle registration	—	Yes	—	No
Option for products liability litigation	Yes	Yes	Yes	No
Adapts existing insurance framework	Yes	Yes	Yes	Yes

[a] Subject to limits in the auto insurance policy.

CHAPTER FIVE

Assessing the Impact That Technologies for Autonomous Vehicles Can Have on Auto Insurance Policies, the Auto Insurance Framework, and Consumer Acceptance

In this chapter, we explore several topics: potential changes to auto insurance policies occasioned by AV technologies, the impact these changes could have on auto insurance frameworks, and the importance that consumer attitudes have for the acceptance of AV technologies and the pace of change in auto insurance. Although provisions for coverage and compensation of injuries sustained in accidents are key aspects of auto insurance policies, as illustrated in Chapters Three and Four, the experts we interviewed highlighted changes to auto insurance policies that could affect both insurers and policy holders in the near future. For example, we asked experts whether minor accidents and fender benders would become significantly more expensive because of the cost of repairing the sensors in AVs or whether this concern has been overblown.

In our interviews, we discussed the impact of various risks, such as cyberattacks. We asked experts whether it was likely that software updates for technologies for automated vehicles and AVs would be the responsibility of an individual policy holder or fleet owner in the future. Experts also shared their views on liability for cyberattacks on AVs and the potential risks for insurers and considered the potential liability of remote operators. For this chapter, we considered how these potential changes to auto insurance policies and coverage might be handled by the five insurance frameworks that we have discussed previously:

- national no-fault insurance
- state no-fault insurance
- self-insurance by manufacturers
- fleet insurance policies
- adaptation of the existing automobile insurance framework.

Informed by our interviews with industry stakeholders, we also considered the future of data-sharing between OEMs and insurance companies. Finally, we examined expert perspectives on the importance of consumer acceptance of AVs, in response to our research question.

Will New Technologies for Autonomous Vehicles Increase the Cost of Auto Insurance?

In previous chapters, we have discussed whether the current U.S. auto insurance framework would continue into the foreseeable future if it were able to accommodate the new technologies associated with AVs. An important aspect of this adaptability is new costs that might accompany new technologies and how these costs could affect insurers and auto insurance. Auto insurance coverage in the future will need to address losses related to the repair and replacement of critical technologies used in automated vehicles and AVs, such as sensors, video cameras, lidar, and radar. Automated vehicles and AVs use these technologies for perceiving and understanding their environment and providing fail safe operation.[1] As illustrated in Figure 5.1, sensors, video cameras, lidar, and radar may be located on different parts of a vehicle.

The new technologies used in automated vehicles and AVs can provide, for example, the following capabilities, also illustrated in Figure 5.2:

- adaptive cruise control
- traffic sign recognition
- emergency braking
- collision detection
- lane departure warning
- digital side mirror surround view
- environment mapping
- blind-spot detection
- rear collision warning
- park assistance surround view
- rear view.

Many of these capabilities are already included in recent models of vehicles. To understand the effect that these capabilities can have on repair costs and the claims process, we asked experts whether minor accidents and fender benders would become significantly more expensive because of the cost of repairing the sensors in AVs or whether this concern has been overblown.

Experts were generally in agreement that the sensors used by AV technologies would increase the cost of accidents involving AVs, at least initially. They differed, however, in their assessments of the extent of this impact. At present, experts told us, sensors often reside behind the bumpers of AVs and vehicles with driver assistance technologies (see also NHTSA, undated b), as well as in the windshields of these vehicles. Sensors provide AVs the ability to perceive and interpret their surround-

---

[1] When discussing some of the activities that automated technologies perform and capabilities that they provide, we take the liberty of anthropomorphizing a bit, for ease of discussion.

Figure 5.1
Locations of Technology Implementations for Autonomous Vehicles

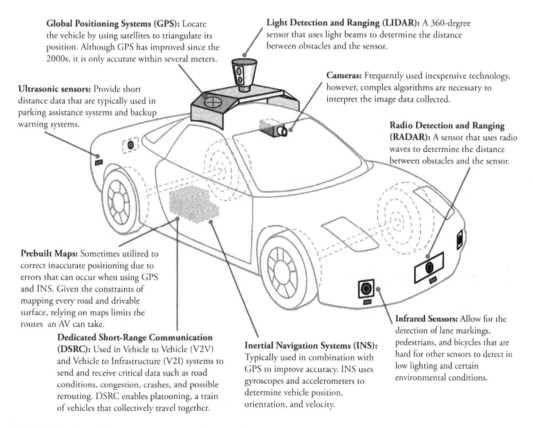

Global Positioning Systems (GPS): Locate the vehicle by using satellites to triangulate its position. Although GPS has improved since the 2000s, it is only accurate within several meters.

Light Detection and Ranging (LIDAR): A 360-degree sensor that uses light beams to determine the distance between obstacles and the sensor.

Ultrasonic sensors: Provide short distance data that are typically used in parking assistance systems and backup warning systems.

Cameras: Frequently used inexpensive technology, however, complex algorithms are necessary to interpret the image data collected.

Radio Detection and Ranging (RADAR): A sensor that uses radio waves to determine the distance between obstacles and the sensor.

Prebuilt Maps: Sometimes utilized to correct inaccurate positioning due to errors that can occur when using GPS and INS. Given the constraints of mapping every road and drivable surface, relying on maps limits the routes an AV can take.

Dedicated Short-Range Communication (DSRC): Used in Vehicle to Vehicle (V2V) and Vehicle to Infrastructure (V2I) systems to send and receive critical data such as road conditions, congestion, crashes, and possible rerouting. DSRC enables platooning, a train of vehicles that collectively travel together.

Inertial Navigation Systems (INS): Typically used in combination with GPS to improve accuracy. INS uses gyroscopes and accelerometers to determine vehicle position, orientation, and velocity.

Infrared Sensors: Allow for the detection of lane markings, pedestrians, and bicycles that are hard for other sensors to detect in low lighting and certain environmental conditions.

SOURCES: Adapted from T. S., 2015, and Center for Sustainable Systems, 2016, p. 1. Used with permission.

ings, including road markings and signage, and are therefore vital to the operation of the automation. Sensors can be very expensive, costing many thousands of dollars to replace or recalibrate.

The expensive nature of AVs' sensors has important implications for the repair industry. The auto repair industry is part of the "crash economy" that includes hospital emergency rooms and insurance claim adjusters (Anderson, Kalra, Stanley, Sorensen, et al., 2016). The crash economy for auto insurance has been described in the following way:

> The transition to AVs is likely to cause considerable economic disruption in other ways as well. American consumers spend approximately $157 billion in automobile insurance premiums every year (U.S. Census Bureau, [2011], p. 755 [Section 25, Table 1222]). This supports not only insurance companies, but also doctors, lawyers, trauma centers, body shops, chiropractors and many others—an entire "crash economy." Automobile insurance companies are also important investors in fed-

Figure 5.2
The Functionalities of Technologies for Automating Vehicles

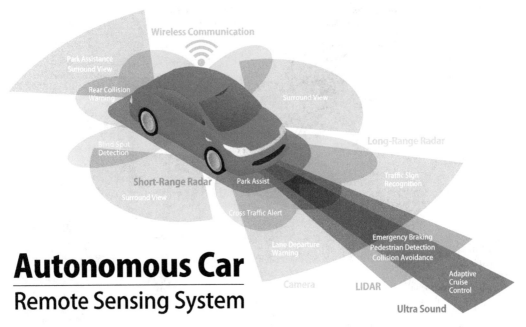

Autonomous Car
Remote Sensing System

Credit: metamorworks/AdobeStock.

eral, state, and municipal bonds. This entire sector of the economy may well be remade as crashes, and the wealth transfers they occasion, decline in frequency. (Anderson, Kalra, Stanley, Sorensen, et al., 2016, pp. 39–40)

In the future, some of the experts we interviewed told us, repairing AVs and, in particular, their sensors may be restricted to highly specialized repair shops, which could result in more-expensive repairs. For this reason, a fender bender involving an AV might cost many thousands of dollars to repair—exponentially higher than the current cost of repairs after a low-speed accident involving conventional cars. Insurance experts indicated that, currently, such low-speed accidents are a large proportion of the auto insurance claims that are filed each year and characterized them as the "bread and butter" of auto insurance claims. A trucking fleet expert concurred that the financial consequences of low-speed accidents would increase because the sensors in AVs, including trucks, are more expensive than the instrumentation in older, conventional vehicles. One stakeholder told us that a low-speed accident in a parking lot might "total" an AV, meaning that the cost to repair the car would exceed its value. Several insurance company experts pointed out their efforts to convince manufacturers to place sensors in more-protected locations, such as the wheel wells.

Other experts minimized the potential impact of the cost of sensors and sensor repair, stating that vehicles that possess technologies to operate at Levels 4 and 5 are going to be involved in fewer collisions because of the sensor technology embedded in them and that, therefore, the overall cost to the industry would probably be about equal to what it is today. For example, one manufacturer interviewee explained that the "decreased frequency [of collisions] will offset the increased severity in the upcoming years." An insurance industry stakeholder disagreed with this assessment, however, explaining that "loss severity is a significant issue" and that, "even if there's a decrease in [the number of] crashes, the loss severity will go up." Several experts predicted that, although sensors are expensive now, as they become a more common feature, their cost would decrease. One expert explained that the price of sensors would "decrease dramatically" thanks to economies of scale. Other experts pointed out that manufacturers are now putting sensors in windshields and places other than bumpers.

At least two of the industry experts we interviewed had a different perspective on the effect that expensive sensors would have on loss severity. One stated that sensors are meant to be self-calibrating and that "there's a lot of fear mongering" with respect to expensive sensors. Another expert reminded us that expensive sensors are not unique to AVs; many new vehicles with automated technologies now have many of these sensors, too. In summary, the replacement cost of sensors after an accident appears to be a factor that could increase the severity of the loss for insurers and increase costs for owners of AVs, at least initially.

Will the Risk of Cyberattack on Autonomous Vehicles Change Auto Insurance Policies in the Future?

A major concern among industry stakeholders and consumers is the possibility of a malicious actor creating mayhem by hacking into networked AVs. The risk would be that a hacker could take control of many AVs at one time and create widespread damage and perhaps death on the roadways. Another risk scenario involves the hacking of an individual vehicle and the liability for damage caused by the hacker. Among experts interviewed for this study, there was a general consensus that there would be greater demand for cybersecurity risk insurance for automobiles in the future. The experts explained that, because insurance products are generally created by analyzing existing data and creating loss projections, it has been difficult to create cyberinsurance projections for AVs. Several stakeholders we interviewed were unaware that cyberinsurance products for events arising out of the operation of automobiles were currently on the market, but others had heard of cybersecurity insurance policies for automobiles, including policies offered by AIG and other insurance companies.[2] Representatives of one insurance company explained that the availability of cybersecurity insurance

---

[2]   According to experts, the target audience for these cybersecurity policies would be "only the most-sophisticated organizations," such as a fleet operator, which could face a situation in which its fleet is disabled and the operator is required to pay a ransom.

policies would increase as networked vehicles become more common. One insurance expert suggested that, in the future, auto insurance policies might have cybersecurity riders. Several experts cautioned that cybersecurity policies and riders were likely to be very expensive because they involve catastrophic peril. Overall, however, insurers were confident that they could handle future demand for cybersecurity insurance. One insurance company representative explained, "Our industry is good at building these things out, and we're already in the process of doing that."

In discussing the role of manufacturers in setting cybersecurity standards for AVs, one insurance expert questioned whether those standards would be sufficiently rigorous. The international experts we interviewed provided different perspectives on how insurance products might address cybersecurity risk. For example, in Japan, the mandatory scheme will cover cybersecurity intrusions as a matter of course. In the UK, current cybersecurity guidelines cover all connected vehicles, including AVs—a reminder that cyberrisk will increase not just with the rise of AVs but also with the increasing connectedness of conventional cars. Other experts concurred with this view, noting that cyberintrusions are a current threat because of the vulnerability of existing infotainment systems.

In spite of these challenges, however, insurance experts were confident that the automobile insurance industry would be able to create a product to adequately address cyberrisks.

How Might Software Updates for Autonomous Vehicles Reduce Their Insurance Risk?

One of the important methods for reducing cyberrisk, according to industry experts, is compliance with software updates. AVs will require frequent software updates to improve their safety functions, performance, and cybersecurity protections over time. Software updates might be delivered over the air (OTA), similar to how smartphone updates are delivered and installed, or might be installed at a dealership. For example, Tesla currently provides frequent OTA software updates. Although OTA updates might be easier for consumers and reach a larger number of vehicles than dealership-installed software updates would, the cybersecurity risk would probably be higher.

Industry experts explained that software updates are one of the reasons that AVs might be deployed in fleets. Fleet maintenance is considered to be more consistent and reliable than software updates installed by individual vehicle owners. In the UK, if an individual owner of an AV were to alter the vehicle's software or deliberately refuse to update it, that owner would be deemed contributorily negligent in a crash. However, U.S. insurance experts viewed this approach as misguided and unrealistic, noting that it placed too much responsibility on consumers, especially given that "convenience outweighs responsibility." One expert suggested that the states could play a role in monitoring software updates, just as some states currently require annual car inspections. Checking compliance with software updates could be part of such annual inspections. One stakeholder noted, "States may play a role in inspecting AVs," and "there must be an opportunity to ensure that the software is kept up to date." An approach in which individual owners would be found contributorily negligent for having less than the latest software installed has its limitations, however: Given that AVs require frequent software updates, annual inspections would provide only occasional oversight, and not every state requires inspections. One expert questioned how often state regulators would need to approve updated software systems and how much of the approval process would need to be repeated for successive updates.[3] Another stakeholder observed, similarly, "If state regulators approve the initial system, how much of the approval process needs to be repeated for each successive software update?"

Again, international models may provide some guidance. In the UK, for example, an AV owner must update a centralized registry if there are changes to the vehicle's software. Both U.S. and non-U.S. experts noted that it is important to know what version of software was being used at the time of an accident to aid in accident reconstruction and determination of liability. One stakeholder concluded that software updates "are a concern" and that "data recorders are important here" because "they will show what version of software was in use."

How Will Data on Autonomous Vehicles Contribute to Auto Insurance?

Although AV technologies have advanced significantly in recent years, considerable uncertainty exists about how the very large amounts of data produced by AVs could, and should, be shared among OEMs, auto insurance companies, and other stakeholders. It is difficult to identify any generally accepted definition of the types of data that may be gathered, produced, or transmitted by AVs. The Telematics Task Force identified the following types of data in AV systems:

- Driver personal data—includes passwords, [account numbers], phone numbers, logins, geolocation data, personal history, biometrics, driver behavior, etc.
- In Vehicle Infotainment—includes songs, movies, games, maps, applications and other third party copyrighted material.
- Forensic information—data used by car companies, legal entities and insurance companies, etc. to determine driving parameters following a crash. It also can include any information gleaned from a vehicle following any crime where the vehicle can reveal evidence, even the driver's personal data.

---

[3]   One insurance expert noted in comments to the authors provided April 1, 2020, that the manufacturer could make operation of the vehicle conditional on software updates. If an update is safety critical, the vehicle could be bricked until the software is updated. It may be necessary, according to the expert, to clarify this through state legislation.

- Inspection data—includes emissions and safety related data and codes used for official periodic inspections.
- Diagnostic data—Codes and [parameter identifiers] used to diagnose vehicle faults. This also includes prognosis information including oil quality monitors and other data used to predict or communicate service scheduling.
- Vehicle Manufacturer (VM) proprietary information—includes onboard software, some security related information as well as calibration information. Calibration files contain vehicle configuration data, for example, upper and lower operating limits, code setting thresholds and other data unique to a specific year, make, model and engine configuration.
- Intelligent Transport Systems (ITS) Information—includes GPS, radar, sonar, yaw and accelerometer information used for Vehicle to Vehicle (V2V) and Vehicle to Infrastructure (V2I) communications. (Telematics Task Force, 2014, p. 1; see also Stanley and Wagner, 2015, p. 3)

The sharing of these data is complicated by the fact that the data may contain personally identifiable information. A key issue for many AV stakeholders, especially insurance companies and OEMs, is what data will be shared and how.

Currently, there is no established framework for OEMs to provide auto insurance providers data that might be relevant to insurance claims, although insurance companies contend that they need access to these data to pay claims and assess the risks posed by AVs.[4] At a RAND workshop in July 2016, "Rethinking Insurance and Liability in the Transformative Age of Autonomous Vehicles," representatives of manufacturers and insurers discussed this issue. A workshop participant stated that the top-priority public policy issue for the insurance industry was the relevance and importance of data access (Anderson, Kalra, Stanley, and Morikawa, 2018, pp. 7–8). The workshop participant "explained that data help build out the framework of regulation and confirm that the technology works as advertised" (p. 6). However, he said, "when the insurance industry raises the issue of access to AV data, . . . the response from manufacturers is 'that's proprietary'" (p. 6). He added that "data are the key to everything, and it is impossible to tease apart safety data from other data that are important to companies on a proprietary level, such as data usage" (p. 6). The workshop participant concluded that "all stakeholders are thinking about data—and everyone is guarding them" (p. 6).

Another workshop participant explained that, "for the insurance world, data are used to resolve claims" (Anderson, Kalra, Stanley, and Morikawa, 2018, p. 7). He noted that "the data may be proprietary, but they are still needed to pay off claims" (p. 7). He concluded that it "was incumbent on the insurance industry to determine how to reduce friction in the claims system." Our interviews with experts for this study confirmed that there is still considerable tension between manufacturers and insurers

---

[4]   As one insurance expert noted in correspondence dated March 18, 2020, "[T]his refers to losses, accidents or malfunctions, because there are no insurance claims unless/until policies are issued—and policies aren't issued unless/until the premium is established, dependent on loss/accident data or other relevant proxies."

stemming from the issue of data-sharing. One manufacturer, for example, character-ized auto insurance companies as "data hungry." In general, OEMs are reluctant to share potentially proprietary and confidential data. As one academic noted, OEMs "run on trade secrets." An AV manufacturer explained, "I don't think it is in the man-ufacturer's business interest to give them this data just because they're too lazy to do it themselves. . . . [T]hey have plenty of ways to get the data." This perception—that manufacturers do not have a responsibility to share AV data—was common in our interviews. Another manufacturer told us that it was "way premature" for insurance companies to obtain AV data from manufacturers, explaining, "We think what the insurance companies are asking for isn't going to be available for quite some time. Later on, if they're not getting the information they want, we can discuss that." A study of legal aspects of AVs for the Transportation Research Board concluded,

> Whether rating driverless cars under a personal liability regime or a products liabil-ity regime, insurers will be challenged by lack of data. Testing data and simulations are helpful, but they are a poor substitute for actual data generated by the driving of these vehicles in the hands of the public. (National Academies of Sciences, Engi-neering, and Medicine, 2016, p. 60)

In contrast to the friction between manufacturers and insurers about AV data, vehicle owners indicated that they would be willing to share their vehicle data. Survey research on AV issues conducted in 2018 by J. D. Power reported, "When respondents were asked if they would be willing to share vehicle data, including video information from the cameras, 74% said they 'definitely' or 'probably would' share this informa-tion" (Westenberg et al., 2018, p. 44).

The authors of the J. D. Power report concluded that

> there was a substantial consensus that information should be shared for the greater good of developing automated vehicles. Respondents willing to share vehicle data expressed an overwhelming desire to help manufacturers and designers, improve future technology, avoid accidents, lower insurance premiums, determine cause or fault, improve safety, and in general help the "next guy" . . . . (Westenberg et al., 2018, p. 45).

Given the lack of clarity about AV data-sharing and its importance to the devel-opment of AV, federal regulators are monitoring the issue in the AV industry. If neces-sary, they could seek to facilitate data-sharing. Meanwhile, U.S. cities and local transit agencies are actively exploring ways to encourage the sharing of AV data. Although there is no current consensus regarding a way forward for AV data-sharing between and among vehicle owners, manufacturers, and the insurance industry, there are ongo-ing efforts to address this issue. Although an assessment of collection and sharing of AV data exceeds the scope of this report, our interviews confirmed that the development of standards for collection and sharing of AV data among stakeholders is an important topic for further research.[5]

Are Remote Operators "Drivers" Under a Commercial Auto Insurance Policy?

We also considered the potential liability issues associated with regulations that require remote operators for testing AVs. In California, for example, manufacturers are required to have a two-way communication link between an autonomous test vehicle and a remote operator. This means that there may be a passenger or observer in the AV while there is also an always-on connection to a remote operator at a network operating center. Our understanding is that some companies, such as Waymo, use remote operators in testing their vehicles (see, e.g., Heaney555, 2019). These remote operators might supply information to the autonomous test vehicle but cannot take over vehicle control (see, e.g., Heaney555, 2019). In contrast, remote operators at some companies, such as Phantom Auto, can take over AV operations remotely (Higgins, 2018).

The California Code of Regulations provides, in pertinent part,

> (b) The manufacturer certifies that the autonomous test vehicle complies with the all of the following:
>
> (1) There is a communication link between the vehicle and the remote operator to provide information on the vehicle's location and status and allow two-way communication between the remote operator and any passengers if the vehicle experiences any failures that would endanger the safety of the vehicle's passengers or other road users, or otherwise prevent the vehicle from functioning as intended, while operating without a driver. The certification shall include:
>
> > (A) That the manufacturer will continuously monitor the status of the vehicle and the two-way communication link while the autonomous test vehicle is being operated without a driver;
> >
> > (B) A description of how the manufacturer will monitor the communication link; and,
> >
> > (C) An explanation of how all of the vehicles tested by the manufacturer will be monitored.

---

[5]   The experts we interviewed were knowledgeable about insurance, law, and policy issues; they were not experts in the development of standards for AV data. See also "Lax U.S. Oversight of Industry Jeopardizes Public Safety," 2018, p. 11.

(2) There is a process to display or communicate vehicle owner or operator information as specified in Vehicle Code section 16025 in the event that the vehicle is involved in a collision or if there is a need to provide that information to a law enforcement officer for any reason. (Cal. Code Regs. Tit. 13, § 227.38)

Among the industry experts we interviewed, there was a consensus that existing legal frameworks are sufficient to determine the liability of remote operators. For example, they suggested that a remote operator could be treated as an independent contractor of the company testing the AV. One expert suggested that, if a city employed a remote operator, the city would be liable for the remote operator's actions, just as if the operator were a bus driver. At the same time, some experts thought, a new framework was needed for thinking about liability issues surrounding remote operators. An expert on state regulation of AVs suggested that states could require remote operators to be licensed. Another important regulatory issue is the number of vehicles a remote operator might be permitted to monitor at one time. From our interviews, it is not clear whether remote operators will become more prevalent as AVs are deployed or whether their use will be limited to testing phases. A National Academies of Sciences, Engineering, and Medicine study of legal issues relevant to AVs distinguished AVs from vehicles that may be controlled remotely by an external operator; the authors wrote,

Remote control over a vehicle by an external operator does not make the vehicle driverless. Although no human driver may be present in the vehicle, a remotely controlled vehicle does not control its own operation. Control by external operators simply moves the vehicle's "driver" from being a human inside the vehicle to someone outside the vehicle. (National Academies of Sciences, Engineering, and Medicine, 2016, p. 28)

Following the logic of the distinction made in the National Academies report, the liability of remote operators for the testing of AVs might be that of a "driver" employed by a manufacturer or commercial entity who is covered by a commercial insurance policy. Currently, remote operators are engaged in testing automated vehicles and AVs; they are employees of AV manufacturers, or, perhaps, they are independent contractors retained for this specific purpose. If a remote operator is an employee of an AV manufacturer, engaged in work within the scope of employment, the operator would presumably be covered by the manufacturer's commercial insurance policy. If the remote operator is an independent contractor, coverage might come from the commercial insurance of another employer or from the operator's own commercial insurance policy. However, whether remote operators would be treated as drivers, with the attendant legal liability in the event of an AV accident, remains unclear.[6] As we discussed

---

[6] On February 4, 2016, Reuters reported about NHTSA's response to a letter from Google about the definition of *driver* on an AV:

in Chapter Two, automation makes it more likely that the driver is not the "cheapest cost avoider." As the driver does less and the automation more, it probably makes less sense to impose liability on the driver in the hope of creating incentives to reduce accident costs. The car is doing more; the driver less. This is particularly true at Level 4 or 5, when the automation has assumed the driving task and the human driver has little control over how the automation executes the driving task. Or to put it another way, there is little deterrence created by placing liability on the driver if the driver does not have much control over the factors that create crashes or accidents.

How Important Is Consumer Acceptance to the Deployment of Autonomous Vehicles?

When we asked experts to assess the importance of consumer acceptance for the adoption of AVs, all of them indicated that consumer acceptance is "very important."

An AV start-up representative told us that the "main thing that we are cognizant of is that this is a nascent industry, and one thing that's really important is consumer trust. We don't want to impede the adoption of this technology."

Researchers on a previous RAND study warned that, without consumer acceptance, the market for AVs could fail (Anderson, Kalra, Stanley, Sorensen, et al., 2016, p. 136; but see Xu and Fan, 2019 [finding high acceptance of AVs in China]). Market failure would mean that a new framework for auto insurance would not be necessary and that the existing auto insurance framework would not need to be adapted for AVs. Market failure would affect not only the OEMs and many companies that have invested millions of dollars in developing AV technologies; it could potentially result in a negative social outcome—injuries and lives lost in automobile crashes that might have been prevented if consumers had adopted AV technologies on a widespread basis. An expert from an OEM explained,

> Consumer acceptance will be critical to the technology. If consumers don't think that the technology can get them from point A to point B, all the resources that have been invested will be wasted. The safe deployment of these vehicles in the public is the best way to show the public that these are safe and reliable ways to get around. This is one advantage of the rideshare model.

The RAND report concluded,

Google's self-driving car unit on Nov. 12 submitted a proposed design for a self-driving car that has "no need for a human driver," the letter to Google from National Highway Traffic Safety Administration Chief Counsel Paul Hemmersbaugh said.

"NHTSA will interpret 'driver' in the context of Google's described motor vehicle design as referring to the (self-driving system), and not to any of the vehicle occupants," NHTSA's letter said. (Shepardson and Lienert, 2016)

Despite the current enthusiasm for AV technology and the amount of research among automakers and others, it is possible that it will not become widely adopted, simply because it will be too expensive. Absent sufficient demand, economies of scale and network effects will not reduce the marginal cost and the technology might wither. The lack of a viable business model has doomed some earlier efforts at road vehicle automation. (Anderson, Kalra, Stanley, Sorensen, et al., 2016, p. 136)

The expense of the sensors described previously in this chapter and the cost of other technologies used on AVs could contribute to such market failure. The previous report stated,

One important uncertainty is the precise business model for selling this technology to consumers. Many of the existing demonstrations of AV technology involve suites of sensors that currently cost tens of thousands of dollars and would double or triple the cost of most cars. It seems unlikely that consumer demand would be substantial at such a cost. (Anderson, Kalra, Stanley, Sorensen, et al., 2016, p. 136)

It may be that the initial deployment of AVs in fleets, as the majority of the experts we interviewed thought was a likely situation, would address the issue of direct cost to consumers. However, if AVs are very expensive, at least initially, plus require expensive maintenance, even a shared mobility model may prove to be too expensive for many consumers to experience the potential benefits of AV technologies. The authors of the previous RAND report concluded that policymakers might consider a combination of subsidies and taxes to prevent market failure, if the potential benefits of AV technologies are judged to have the potential to substantially benefit social welfare (Anderson, Kalra, Stanley, Sorensen, et al., 2016, p. xxiv).

The 2018 report by J. D. Power and the law firm of Miller Canfield stated that survey research by J. D. Power demonstrated increasing consumer skepticism about AVs and the need for auto industry messaging and education:

The level of consumer trust with fully automated self-driving vehicles, or ADS, is currently in a year-over-year decline. In the *J.D. Power 2017 U.S. Tech Choice Study,*[SM] consumers displayed more skepticism and a growing level, with more saying they either "definitely would not" or "probably would not" trust the technology. Concerns over vehicles being hacked, technology complexity, and what happens if the automated vehicle technology fails are top of mind for consumers. There is a missing link between the lower levels of automation technology on the road today vs. the vehicle taking full driving control. Such concerns show the importance of the industry messaging, including education, regarding what these technologies can and cannot do and essentially what it will mean for the driver. (Westenberg et al., 2018, p. 30)

One of the national experts we interviewed had a different perspective on consumer acceptance, relating consumer acceptance to greater knowledge of and experience with AVs:

> It's difficult for consumers to say how they would react without being really well informed. I heard someone say that consumer acceptance was low, but if we gave out a survey in 1902, they'd probably be pretty happy with their horse and buggy. We have to be careful about consumer acceptance if the consumer doesn't know [all of the details about the product].

This view of consumer acceptance is supported by an observation in the 2018 report by J. D. Power and Miller Canfield, which indicated,

> There has been a notable shift since the January 2017 research findings of the *U.S. Tech Choice Study*, where a substantial number of Pre-Boomers, Baby Boomers, and Gen X did not see any benefits (44%, 40%, and 29%, respectively). Such shifts in opinion will likely continue to occur as consumers become more educated about all aspects of automated driving, witness it in action, and experience firsthand lower levels of automation. (Westenberg et al., 2018, p. 40)

In summary, consumer acceptance appears to be an important factor in the widespread adoption and deployment of AVs. The pace of consumer acceptance of AVs could affect the need to adapt the existing auto insurance framework or adopt a new one, as discussed in previous chapters.

How Might Different Auto Insurance Frameworks Accommodate Technologies for Autonomous Vehicles?

In our interviews with industry experts, we explored how the five auto insurance frameworks that are discussed in previous chapters might accommodate the challenges described in this chapter. The list of challenges described in this chapter is not exhaustive. Rather, it is illustrative of the issues that will need to be addressed by auto insurance frameworks in the future. We discussed five frameworks here:

- national no-fault insurance
- state no-fault insurance
- self-insurance by manufacturers
- fleet insurance policies
- adaptation of the existing automobile insurance framework.

For illustrative purposes, we compared the five frameworks on the following characteristics: (1) the ability to accommodate the cost of new technologies; (2) the ability to address the risk of cyberattacks; (3) the ability to address liability issues around software updates; (4) the ability to use AV data; (5) the ability to provide coverage for new entities involved with AVs, such as "remote operators"; and (6) consumer acceptance.

National no-fault insurance might not prove very flexible in incorporating new and changing costs of technologies used in the repair of AVs. However, it could be a useful way to address the significant financial impact of a large-scale cyberattack. Given its statutory construction, it might be difficult for such a framework to address developments in liability issues around the use of software updates and such concepts as *remote operator*, unless these topics were specifically included in statutory language. A national no-fault framework probably would not need AV data to determine liability or pay claims. A national no-fault insurance framework might have an impact on consumer acceptance of AVs by reassuring consumers that they would be compensated in case of loss or injury, similar to the way national no-fault insurance frameworks function for vaccines and the nuclear industry.

The most common model of no-fault insurance in use in U.S. states *should* have the ability to accommodate the cost of new technologies, such as sensors, for repairs after accidents. The framework could also effectively address damage as a result of a cyberattack, given that liability would not need to be established. Similarly, issues of liability related to software updates and remote operators would not create a limiting factor for no-fault insurance. A no-fault framework probably would not need AV data to determine liability or to pay claims. A no-fault insurance framework might be appealing to some consumers; however, limits on coverage under no-fault insurance policies might lead to litigation. Consumers might resist no-fault insurance if it is perceived as more expensive or as promoting fraud, as indicated by several of the experts we interviewed.

Self-insurance by manufacturers is difficult to assess. If a manufacturer incorporated an established auto insurance company as part of its AV sales operations, as several of the experts we interviewed suggested, its ability to incorporate the costs of new and changing technologies, create policies to deal with cyberattacks, and assess newly emerging liability issues, such as noncompliance with software updates and whether a remote operator is a driver, might be equivalent to traditional auto insurance providers. If manufacturers decide to establish their own auto insurance organization, it is unknown how they might handle these challenges. Consumer acceptance, however, might be enhanced if manufacturers bundled insurance with the sale of AVs, according to several of the experts we interviewed.

Fleet insurance policies for AVs would presumably be based on existing fleet insurance models. These policies are able to incorporate the cost of new and changing technologies, determine coverage for events (such as cyberattacks), and assess newly emerging liability issues. Consumer acceptance of AVs employed in a fleet might be enhanced by the inclusion of insurance as part of the cost of use, according to several experts we interviewed.

Adaptation of the existing auto insurance framework would permit accommodation of the cost of new and changing technologies, could create policies to deal with cyberattacks, could assess newly emerging liability issues (such as noncompliance with software updates and whether a remote operator is a driver), and could include AV data to improve the claims process. The consumer acceptance of AVs might set the pace for how swiftly these changes would need to be incorporated into the existing auto insurance framework. One of the experts we interviewed stated, "You want a system where you can resolve these claims quickly, and consumers can get their cars fixed quickly, and adjusters can move onto the next claim."

In summary, this chapter has explored whether new AV technologies will increase the cost of auto insurance, whether the risk of cyberattack on AVs will change auto insurance policies of the future, how software updates might reduce the insurance risk for AVs in the future, and how AV data could contribute to auto insurance. In addition, we have considered whether remote operators could be drivers under a commercial auto insurance policy. We have also examined the importance of consumer acceptance to the deployment of AVs and determined that it is an important factor that might set the pace for new or adaptive auto insurance frameworks. Finally, we have illustrated how different auto insurance frameworks might accommodate some specific issues related to AV technologies.

CHAPTER SIX

Findings and Recommendations

Findings

In this chapter, we organize our main findings in accordance with the nine research questions that animated this report.

Will the introduction of vehicles that have Level 4 or 5 autonomous capabilities require significant changes to the existing U.S. automobile insurance system, or is the current insurance model flexible enough to handle vehicles that incorporate technologies that permit autonomous operation at most or all times? The majority of U.S. stakeholders, representing both manufacturers and the insurance industry, expressed optimism that the existing insurance framework would be able to adapt to the deployment of AVs (see Table 3.3 in Chapter Three). As one manufacturer interviewee told us, there is "no reason that the current system cannot keep working." Experts noted the historical resilience of the insurance industry in the face of persistent technological innovation.

Less than half of the experts who thought that the current auto insurance framework would persist suggested that the existing automobile insurance system in the United States would not be able to adapt to AVs. Several of these experts indicated that, when a vehicle is operating autonomously, liability will have to shift away from the driver and the cost of insurance will be bundled with the vehicle.

However, a large majority of stakeholders, including those who anticipated changes in the insurance industry, thought that the status quo would persist for the foreseeable future (see Table 3.3 in Chapter Three). Those who foresaw changes in the industry were split as to whether those changes would occur at Level 3 or 4, with the majority asserting that changes would occur at Level 4. One insurance industry expert observed, "It's going to be a sloppy transition; it's not going to happen all at once."

What are the benefits and drawbacks of potential future models for automobile insurance? The criteria that the experts we interviewed used to define benefits and drawbacks of future models for auto insurance were

- whether legislative action would be required
- potential incentive or disincentive for manufacturer safety improvements

- fraud concerns
- ease of the claims process
- application to all levels of automation.

The experts discussed the potential benefits of current state no-fault and national no-fault insurance as possible future models for auto insurance. A large majority of the experts we interviewed dismissed the idea of national no-fault insurance as impractical because it would require congressional legislation and because a government-run claims system was perceived to be unwieldy and unlikely to swiftly provide compensation for the injured (see Table 3.1 in Chapter Three).

Although some experts thought that, in a future in which most vehicles on the road have Level 4 capabilities, a state no-fault framework might be beneficial and easy, the majority of experts rejected the idea of adopting the current state no-fault system in the future (see Table 3.1 in Chapter Three). This was primarily due, as the experts expressed, to their concern that a state no-fault system would fail to provide adequate incentive for manufacturers to improve their AVs.

Self-insurance by manufacturers of AVs had several proponents. These experts thought that OEMs might purchase insurance companies and have them handle the insurance for their AVs. According to several experts, this would allow OEMs to bundle insurance with the sale of AVs, which might provide the benefit of indicating to consumers that the OEMs considered their vehicles to be safe. One expert thought that bundling of insurance with the price of an AV might serve as a competitive advantage. Some experts viewed self-insurance by manufacturers skeptically unless an experienced insurance company was involved. The skeptical experts pointed out that auto insurance was not a core competency of OEMs; it requires licensing in 50 states and a smoothly functioning claims process. Many of the stakeholders we interviewed, however, did not express an opinion about self-insurance by manufacturers.

Fleet insurance was acknowledged by a significant majority of the experts as being a likely future model for insuring AVs. Experts commented that it would have the benefit of being based on existing models for fleet insurance, with a well-established claims process to compensate the injured (see Table 3.1 in Chapter Three).

What is the likelihood that AVs will be insured in fleets rather than by individual policy holders? The majority of stakeholders we interviewed expected AVs to be deployed initially in fleets. The insurance industry, we were told, would handle AV fleets "the way they always have." That is, the owners of fleets would choose to self-insure or to purchase insurance under corporate general liability policies. One manufacturer interviewee told us that their company already insures its fleets of nonautonomous vehicles under corporate general liability policies. Existing fleet insurance policies for limousines and taxis provide another model for insuring fleets of AVs in the future. The transition to fleets of AVs is likely to be modeled on this existing approach to insurance. Stakeholders indicated that, under this model, fleet owners should bear responsibility for accidents caused by their AVs.

Is the subrogation process likely to change in future models for automobile insurance? Most stakeholders indicated that the deployment of AVs would not affect subrogation. Subrogation is a "big part of what [insurers] do" today, and insurer interviewees told us that they would continue to handle the subrogation process in the same way. Although the deployment of AVs may create a more complex ecosystem of suppliers and, in some cases, make it more difficult to determine which supplier was at fault, insurers anticipated continuing to "handle this like [they] handle suppliers today." One stakeholder noted, however, that insurers would be less concerned about being able to pursue subrogation against manufacturers that handle all or most hardware and software in-house. The experts explained that the different business models of AV manufacturers would affect the extent to which subrogation remains a common feature of the claims process.

In the future, how might accidents between AVs and conventional vehicles and between AVs and pedestrians be handled? A majority of stakeholders indicated that, for accidents involving AVs and conventional cars, the claims process would not change significantly. In contrast to the claims process, however, one expert indicated that, for an accident involving severe injuries, the injured party might consider suing the AV manufacturer if the losses exceeded the policy limit of the AV driver or owner.

Many stakeholders indicated that accidents between AVs and pedestrians would be handled the same way as those between conventional cars and pedestrians. The experts we interviewed noted that pedestrians care less about the kind of vehicle that harms them than about being compensated for that harm. As one manufacturer interviewee told us, "If I'm a pedestrian and you run me over, I sue under your primary auto policy. If I'm struck by an autonomous vehicle, I sue under the policy of the owner or registrant." Other stakeholders predicted that the severity of accidents involving pedestrians would go down because AVs "won't be speeding and will brake" for pedestrians. Numerous stakeholders indicated that new issues about pedestrians are likely to emerge as AVs are deployed. One expert noted that pedestrians are inherently unpredictable, and AV technologies will need to be developed to "anticipate the unexpected" on busy city streets.

Will minor accidents and fender benders become significantly more expensive because of the cost of repairing the sensors in AVs, or is this concern overblown? The experts we interviewed were generally in agreement that the sensors used by AV technologies would increase the cost of accidents involving AVs, at least initially. Experts differed, however, in their assessments of the extent of this impact. Other experts minimized the potential impact of the cost of sensors and sensor repair, stating that AVs that incorporate technologies that allow them to operate at Levels 4 and 5 would be involved in fewer collisions because of the sensor technology embedded within them and that, therefore, the overall cost to the industry probably would be about equal to what it is today.

How might changes to accommodate AVs in the insurance models of other countries inform changes to U.S. automobile insurance? We investigated the approach to adapting the insurance framework for AVs in four countries: the UK, Australia, Canada, and Japan. We were especially interested in these countries because the primary focus of their insurance frameworks is on compensating the injured. All of the countries have a focus on swift and easy compensation for victims of accidents. For this reason, reliance on products liability litigation was not the most favored approach to victim compensation.[1] All of the countries we investigated followed an adaptive approach to incorporating AVs into auto insurance schemes. The experts we consulted indicated that the current framework for auto insurance would be flexible enough to accommodate AVs up to Level 3 but that, once most vehicles were at Level 4 or Level 5, the auto insurance framework might need to change.

We compared the frameworks of the four countries across ten aspects: (1) ubiquitous coverage of drivers and victims; (2) minimal insurance coverage for all drivers; (3) mandatory insurance; (4) full compensation for victims; (5) applicability to AVs; (6) a national program; (7) paid by insurance premium; (8) paid by vehicle registration; (9) an option for products liability litigation; and (10) adaptation of the existing insurance framework. The framework devised in Australia and the framework proposed in Canada are designed to accommodate states or provinces that have either no-fault or traditional auto insurance, much like in the United States. Each country offered an approach for how full compensation for all victims of an AV accident might be made. In addition, the four countries had innovative approaches to AV data collection and sharing among stakeholders that could inform discussion of this issue in the United States.

How important is consumer acceptance to the deployment of AVs? When we asked experts about the importance of consumer acceptance of AVs, all of them responded that it was "very important." An OEM expert stated,

> Consumer acceptance will be critical to the technology. If consumers don't think that the technology can get them from point A to point B, all the resources that have been invested will be wasted. The safe deployment of these vehicles in the public is the best way to show the public that these are safe and reliable ways to get around.

Survey research by J. D. Power and Miller Canfield underscored the importance of education by the auto industry about AV capabilities in promoting consumer accep-

---

[1] It should be noted that each of these countries has a stronger safety net than in the United States, including more-widespread access to medical insurance, which may explain why there is less reliance on litigation to make victims whole following an accident.

tance. Consumer acceptance appears to be an important factor in the widespread adoption and deployment of AVs. The pace of consumer acceptance of AVs could affect the need to adapt the existing auto insurance framework or adopt a new one.

Will data-sharing between OEMs that produce AVs and insurance companies be important in the future? Currently, there is no established framework for OEMs to provide data pertaining to insurance claims to auto insurance providers, although insurance companies contend that they need access to these data to pay claims and assess the risks posed by AVs.[2] Given the lack of clarity about AV data-sharing and its importance to the development of AVs, federal regulators are monitoring the issue in the AV industry. If necessary, they could seek to facilitate data-sharing. Meanwhile, U.S. cities and local transit agencies are actively exploring ways to encourage the sharing of AV data. Although there is no current consensus regarding a way forward for AV data-sharing between and among vehicle owners, manufacturers, regulators, and the insurance industry, there are ongoing efforts to address this issue. Although an assessment of the collection and sharing of AV data exceeds the scope of this report, our interviews confirmed that the development of standards for collection and sharing of AV data among stakeholders is an important topic for further research.

Recommendations

First, **insurers, manufacturers, and other stakeholders should collaborate to develop a framework for the collection and sharing of data on AVs**. Further research to explore methods for information-sharing between insurers and manufacturers could assist the auto insurance industry in more accurately assessing risk, paying claims, creating new insurance products, and facilitating the adoption of AVs.

Second, **in adapting existing insurance frameworks to accommodate the deployment of AVs, policymakers and insurers in the United States should consider international insurance frameworks**. As discussed in this report, policymakers in the UK, Canada, Japan, Australia, and other countries must also contend with the liability and regulatory implications of the deployment of AVs. Policymakers and insurers in the United States should closely examine these international models, which may provide novel solutions to common liability, coverage, and other issues associated with AVs.

Finally, **further research to understand whether and how the fleet operator model would be likely to help or hinder consumer acceptance would be useful**. Insurance coverage for AVs in different aspects, such as fleet insurance, will play an important role in increasing consumer confidence in these new technologies. Con-

---

[2]   As one insurance expert noted in correspondence dated March 18, 2020, "[T]his refers to losses, accidents or malfunctions, because there are no insurance claims unless/until policies are issued—and policies aren't issued unless/until the premium is established, dependent on loss/accident data or other relevant proxies."

sumer acceptance of AVs will be an important factor in setting the pace for creation of new or adaptive auto insurance frameworks.

Supplement to Chapter Four

The following materials supplement the information provided in Chapter Four about international models that may inform U.S. insurance practices. These materials were supplied by our various international experts following their interviews, as developments occurred in their countries that were relevant to the subject of our study.

The United Kingdom

On October 16, 2019, the UK Law Commission and Scottish Law Commission jointly published *Automated Vehicles: Consultation Paper 2 on Passenger Services and Public Transport.* Comments on the consultation paper were invited from October 16, 2019, to January 16, 2020. See UK Law Commission and Scottish Law Commission, 2019, for copies of the consultation paper and related materials.

The consultation paper states,

> The Centre for Connected and Automated [sic] Vehicles (CCAV) has asked the Law Commission of England and Wales and the Scottish Law Commission to examine options for regulating automated road vehicles. It is a three-year project running from 2018 to 2021.

> Our first consultation paper considered safety assurance together with civil and criminal liability. This paper discusses the regulation of Highly Automated Road Passenger Services (HARPS). We have coined the term HARPS to encapsulate the idea of a new service. It refers to a service which uses self-driving vehicles to provide journeys to passengers without a human driver or user-in-charge. The vehicle would be able to travel empty or with only passengers on board. In other words, there is no person in the vehicle with legal responsibility for its safety.

> In this paper we consider a national licensing scheme for HARPS. We also discuss private ownership of passenger-only vehicles. We cover accessibility for older and disabled people, how to control congestion on public roads and how regulation can help self-driving vehicles integrate with public transport.

The consultation paper notes that the responses to the consultation will inform the next stages of its three-year project. The next review point was scheduled for April 2020, according to the consultation paper. The consultation paper stated that its geographical scope applied to the laws of England, Wales, and Scotland.

Australia

In response to our emailed questions about updates to our original interview, our Australian regulatory expert advised us in October 2019 that, currently, there is compulsory third-party injury insurance in each state and territory in Australia (although programs vary in nature between states). He noted that transport ministers had agreed that there should be a national approach to these schemes and that they should include injuries in crashes involving AVs. He cautioned that the recommendations still need to be agreed to by treasurers (because the regulation of these schemes generally comes under treasury departments rather than transport). He directed us to the policy paper, published in August 2019 by NTC, *Motor Accident Injury Insurance and Automated Vehicles* (NTC, 2019), that requested comments on six options that offered possible avenues for people injured in accidents with AVs to receive compensation. The six options for recovery were originally outlined in the NTC discussion paper published in October 2018 (NTC, 2018) that is discussed in Chapter Four of this report.

The following verbatim excerpt from the NTC policy paper provides amplification for the discussion of the six options for MAII, as discussed in Chapter Four:

Option 1: No changes and rely on the existing legal framework

This option requires a person injured by an ADS to rely on the current legal framework to claim compensation. Claims could be made under existing MAII schemes, the ACL [Australian Consumer Law], negligence or relying on contract law.

This option would not change established processes, but it would result in uncertain and inconsistent outcomes for injured people under MAII schemes. For non-MAII claims, there would likely be delays in accessing compensation, up-front expenses being paid and inconsistent and uncertain outcomes.

Option 2: Exclude injuries caused by an ADS from MAII schemes

This option requires all MAII schemes to exclude cover for injuries caused by an ADS. People injured would not be able to use the MAII schemes to seek compensation and would have to rely on a claim in contract, negligence or the ACL.

This option makes it clear that ADS crashes are not covered by MAII schemes. This option would have similar challenges to option 1, but it provides greater certainty to MAII schemes.

Option 3: Expand MAII schemes to cover injuries caused by an ADS

This option explicitly provides MAII scheme cover for ADS-caused injuries. An injured person could claim compensation regardless of whether injuries were caused by an ADS or a human driver. The option builds on the existing legislative and administrative MAII framework and provides a single point of access for an injured person to claim.

This option could compromise the financial sustainability of MAII schemes if the costs of ADS faults shift from at-fault parties, such as ADSEs to vehicle owners, MAII insurers and governments. Cost-shifting risks could be addressed by:

- insurers exercising a right-of-recovery against at-fault parties (either existing or enhanced right), and/or
- a compulsory reinsurance pool funded by relevant parties who could be responsible for, or contribute to, an ADS fault. MAII schemes would have access to, or a right to recover from, the pool.

Option 4: Purpose-built automated vehicle scheme

This option establishes a separate insurance scheme providing cover for automated vehicles. It could be a national scheme, or a state and territory-based scheme. This option contains ADS liabilities within the automated vehicle supply chain. However, if the scheme was nationally managed, ensuring equitable compensation between automated and non-automated vehicle caused injuries would be complex.

Suggestions were sought from stakeholders on design elements of the scheme.

Option 5: Minimum benchmarks

This option creates agreed national benchmarks for the scope and coverage of ADS crash injuries. States and territories would retain individual responsibility and flexibility to deliver the benchmarks to suit their jurisdictional circumstances. The benchmarks could build upon existing MAII schemes or permit alternative insurance models.

This option will have minimal disruption to existing MAII schemes. However, there may be uncertainty and complexity about how to claim compensation and possibly varied insurance costs for ADSEs.

Option 6: Single insurer

This option allows private insurers to provide personal injury, property damage and other insurance types under a single policy covering all liabilities for an automated vehicle. Jurisdictions that have publicly underwritten MAII schemes would be required to open their market to the private sector (Northern Territory, Tasmania, Victoria, Western Australia).

This option provides the convenience of dealing with one insurer covering all liabilities. It also reduces the exposure of MAII schemes to ADS-related claims. However, insurer costs of pursuing recovery against at-fault parties may ultimately be reflected in premiums paid by automated vehicle owners. A national, single insurer scheme would be difficult to establish given the varied funding of current MAII schemes. (NTC, 2019, pp. 30–31)

The assessment criteria used to perform an initial assessment of the options were as follows:

Will the option ensure a person injured by an ADS is no worse off financially or procedurally than if they were injured by a vehicle controlled by a human driver?

Will the option provide timely payment of claims to injured persons?

Does the option address an identified gap or barrier to personal injury compensation created using automated vehicles?

Will the option send an appropriate price signal to those responsible for the safe operation of automated vehicles to obviate product/system/technology failures and risks?

Is the option capable of accommodating evolving technology, automated vehicles and ownership models? (NTC, 2019, pp. 31–32)

The NTC policy paper states, "The clear majority of stakeholders, representing a variety of sectors, supported option 3" (NTC, 2019, p. 34). The key points that NTC highlighted in its policy paper concerning the six options were as follows:

A consistent, national approach should be taken to provide cover for injuries that result from an ADS crash.

The majority of stakeholders supported expanding existing MAII schemes to cover injuries caused by an ADS. This approach will likely require further work to develop an effective right-of-recovery for insurers.

In the short to medium term cover for injuries should be provided by MAII schemes. The approach should be reviewed by MAII schemes when automated vehicles are a statistically sufficient portion of registered vehicles to enable assessment of their safety risks. (NTC, 2019, p. 30)

Japan

An expert on Japanese legal and regulatory frameworks provided the following update about the request for public comments on the "Safety Standard for Automated Vehicle Apparatus" issued by MLIT. The expert supplied an unofficial but very helpful translation of the safety standards into English. He has asked that we emphasize that the translation is not official and is intended to assist our study. The translation is included here verbatim. The proposed safety standard is particularly interesting in that it requires specific AV data to be recorded and maintained for six months. His unofficial translation follows.

Safety Standard for Automated Vehicle

Issued 2019/12/24

Automatic operation device (Automated driving apparatus)

- While the automatic operation system is in operation, it must not interfere with the safety of passengers and other traffic.
- If the driving environment conditions are not satisfied during operation of the device, a warning is issued to the driver to prompt the driver to take over the driving operation, and the automatic operation system will continue safe operation for a sufficient time to ensure that the driver can take over the driving operation. If it is not taken over by the driver, it will stop safely.
- In principle, the warning shall be given with sufficient time before the driving environment conditions are no longer satisfied.
- If there is a possibility of collision with other traffic or obstacles, the vehicle must be able to avoid collision or apply braking to minimize damage at the collision.
- The system must be able to start and stop by the driver's intentional operation.
- If the driving environment conditions are not satisfied or if there is a possibility that the Automatic operation device may not operate normally, the device shall not operate.
- If there is a risk that the automatic operation device may not operate normally, the driver shall be visually alerted to the driver in the driver's seat.
- The Automatic operation device must have a function that allows the driver to easily and reliably recognize the operation status of the device.

- A function shall be installed to constantly monitor that the driver is ready to take over the driving operation during the operation of the automatic operation device, and to issue an alarm when the driver is not in that state (Driver Monitoring).
- The functions of the automatic operation device shall be designed with redundancy.

Operating status recording device

- The operating status recording device equipped with the automatic operation device shall be capable of recording the following information.
  - Time when the operation status of the Automatic operation device changes.
  - Time when the handover alarm by the automatic operation device was started.
  - The cause of the handover alarm from the automatic operation device.
  - The time when the vehicle equipped with the automatic operation device started the risk minimization control
  - The time when the driver overrode by operating the steering wheel while the automatic operation device was operating
  - A record of the above information shall be retained for at least one of the following short periods:
    - 6 months
    - After the information is recorded, until the above information is recorded more than the number of times that the vehicle has been used for 6 months. (the specific number of times will be specified)

External display

- It will be asked by the ministry notice to the automobile manufacturer that a sticker is attached to indicate that the vehicle is equipped with an automatic operation device that is generally sold and used.

Formulation of guidelines

- Although common international standard understanding has not been obtained at the time of standardization, however, establish guidelines (Record the vehicle behavior and position information when the collision damage mitigation brake is activated during operation of the automatic operation device on the operating status recording device, and equip the automated vehicle with an event data recorder, etc.) which it is desirable to comply with the requirements.

Canada

In response to follow-up questions from our initial interview, one of our Canadian insurance experts explained that no Canadian government or provincial regulator has adopted the single–insurance policy proposal that has been discussed in Canada, but there is interest in the proposal. He provided three related developments that are relevant to our study. In June 2019, our Canadian insurance expert emailed the following explanation to us:

1. In December (2018), the Ontario government amended the automated vehicles pilot project regulation under the Highway Traffic Act [R.S.O. 1990, c. H.8]. With respect to insurance, vehicles in the pilot project, which are SAE levels 4 and 5, require a minimum of $5 million in liability coverage, except for vehicles with a seating capacity of eight or more passengers, which require $8 million. Of note, the insurer providing either level of coverage has to sign a declaration stating that the liability coverage will apply regardless of whether the human operator of the vehicle or the technology is responsible for the collision. This requirement is consistent with the single insurance policy concept, at least for level 4 and 5 vehicles.

2. In February (2019), the Canadian Council of Insurance Regulators (CCIR), which is an association of the provincial insurance regulators, announced that it is studying the current limitations in the insurance laws pertaining to automated vehicles. Studying the current limitations will help the regulators identify future regulatory needs. Currently, CCIR is conducting a gap analysis of the legislation in each province. CCIR will consult with stakeholders in the fall. Following the consultations, CCIR will release an issues paper with its ideas in the spring of 2020.

3. Also in 2019, Transport Canada released Safety Assessment for Automated and Connected Vehicles.[1] The safety assessment is Transport Canada's voluntary guidance. It describes Transport Canada's expectations of vehicle manufacturers that want to sell automated vehicles. Transport Canada will consider the safety assessment when inspecting vehicles and when deciding whether to force corrective measures on vehicle manufacturers.

4. The safety assessment contains a section on data sharing, which is one of the recommendations in IBC's publication. The safety assessment states that vehicle manufacturers "should also consider means to share data on vehicle performance with vehicle owners and/or users upon request (i.e. to support insurance claim processes)" [Transport Canada, 2019, p. 19]. When completing a safety assessment, Transport Canada wants vehicle manufacturers to answer the following questions:
   ○ Are there processes in place to enable data sharing with vehicle owners/operators when requested, for example, to facilitate insurance claims?

---

[1] We believe that he was referring to Transport Canada, 2019.

○ How will vehicle owners be made aware of these processes?

Although the safety assessment is not binding via regulation, the expectation that vehicle manufacturers make collision data available to vehicle owners and other users is a positive development.

Bibliography

Abraham, Kenneth S., and Robert L. Rabin, "Automated Vehicles and Manufacturer Responsibility for Accidents: A New Legal Regime for a New Era," *Virginia Law Review*, Vol. 105, No. 1, March 2019, pp. 127–171.

AEVA—*See* Automated and Electric Vehicles Act 2018.

American Law Institute, *Restatement (Second) of Torts*, Vol. 4, 1979.

Anderson, James M., "The Missing Theory of Variable Selection in the Economic Analysis of Tort Law," *Utah Law Review*, Vol. 2007, No. 2, 2007, pp. 255–285.

Anderson, James M., Paul Heaton, and Stephen J. Carroll, *The U.S. Experience with No-Fault Automobile Insurance: A Retrospective*, Santa Monica, Calif.: RAND Corporation, MG-860-ICJ, 2010. As of October 1, 2020:
https://www.rand.org/pubs/monographs/MG860.html

Anderson, James M., Nidhi Kalra, Karlyn D. Stanley, and Jamie Morikawa, *Rethinking Insurance and Liability in the Transformative Age of Autonomous Vehicles*, Santa Monica, Calif.: RAND Corporation, CF-383-RC, 2018. As of July 20, 2020:
https://www.rand.org/pubs/conf_proceedings/CF383.html

Anderson, James M., Nidhi Kalra, Karlyn D. Stanley, Paul Sorensen, Constantine Samaras, and Tobi A. Oluwatola, *Autonomous Vehicle Technology: A Guide for Policymakers*, Santa Monica, Calif.: RAND Corporation, RR-443-2-RC, 2016. As of November 15, 2020:
https://www.rand.org/pubs/research_reports/RR443-2.html

Aristotle, *Nichomachean Ethics*, Book V, trans. W. D. Ross, written 350 BCE. As of November 15, 2020:
http://classics.mit.edu/Aristotle/nicomachaen.5.v.html

Automated and Electric Vehicles Act 2018, UK Pub. Gen. Acts, 2018 c. 18, 2018. As of June 17, 2019:
https://www.legislation.gov.uk/ukpga/2018/18/contents/enacted

Baker, Tom, "Blood Money, New Money, and the Moral Economy of Tort Law in Action," *Law and Society Review*, Vol. 35, No. 2, 2001, pp. 275–319.

Beale, Alexander F., "Whose Coffers Spill When Autonomous Cars Kill? A New Tort Theory for the Computer Code Road," *Widener Commonwealth Law Review*, Vol. 27, No. 2, 2018, pp. 215–248.

Black, Henry Campbell, ed., *Black's Law Dictionary*, abridged 5th ed., St. Paul, Minn.: West Publishing Company, 1983.

Butcher, Louise, and Tim Edmonds, *Automated and Electric Vehicles Act 2018*, House of Commons Library, research briefing, CBP 8118, August 15, 2018. As of October 1, 2020: https://commonslibrary.parliament.uk/research-briefings/cbp-8118/

Calabresi, Guido, *The Costs of Accidents: A Legal and Economic Analysis*, New Haven and London: Yale University Press, 1970.

California Code of Regulations, Title 13, Motor Vehicles; Division 1, Department of Motor Vehicles; Chapter 1, Department of Motor Vehicles; Article 3.7, Testing of Autonomous Vehicles (Refs and Annos); Section 227.38, Manufacturer's Permit to Test Autonomous Vehicles That Do Not Require a Driver. As of October 7, 2020: https://govt.westlaw.com/calregs/Document/I70962E1666AF4D2B89075856884EA660?viewType=FullText&originationContext=documenttoc&transitionType=CategoryPageItem&contextData=(sc.Default)

Center for Sustainable Systems, University of Michigan, "Autonomous Vehicles," fact sheet, CSS16-18, August 2016. As of October 5, 2020: http://css.umich.edu/factsheets/autonomous-vehicles-factsheet

Coalition Against Insurance Fraud, *The State of Insurance Fraud Technology: A Study of Insurer Use, Strategies and Plans for Anti-Fraud Technology*, Washington, D.C., March 2019. As of October 1, 2020: https://www.sas.com/en/whitepapers/coalition-against-insurance-fraud-the-state-of-insurance-fraud-technology-105976.html

Coase, R. H., "The Problem of Social Cost," *Journal of Law and Economics*, Vol. 3, October 1960, pp. 1–44.

Coleman, Jules L., *The Practice of Principle: In Defence of a Pragmatist Approach to Legal Theory*, Oxford University Press, 2001.

Crane, Daniel A., Kyle D. Logue, and Bryce C. Pilz, "A Survey of Legal Issues Arising from the Deployment of Autonomous and Connected Vehicles," *Michigan Telecommunications and Technology Law Review*, Vol. 23, No. 2, 2017, pp. 191–320.

Dreyer, Paul, Therese Jones, Kelly Klima, Jenny Oberholtzer, Aaron Strong, Jonathan William Welburn, and Zev Winkelman, *Estimating the Global Cost of Cyber Risk: Methodology and Examples*, Santa Monica, Calif.: RAND Corporation, RR-2299-WFHF, 2018. As of October 2, 2020: https://www.rand.org/pubs/research_reports/RR2299.html

Elish, Madeleine Clare, "Moral Crumple Zones: Cautionary Tales in Human–Robot Interaction," *Engaging Science, Technology, and Society*, Vol. 5, 2019, pp. 40–60.

Engstrom, Nora Freeman, "Sunlight and Settlement Mills," *New York University Law Review*, Vol. 86, No. 4, October 2011, pp. 805–886.

———, "An Alternative Explanation for No-Fault's 'Demise,'" *DePaul Law Review*, Vol. 61, No. 2, Winter 2012, pp. 303–382.

———, "A Dose of Reality for Specialized Courts: Lessons from the VICP," *University of Pennsylvania Law Review*, Vol. 163, 2015, pp. 1631–1717.

———, "When Cars Crash: The Automobile's Tort Law Legacy," *Wake Forest Law Review*, Vol. 53, No. 2, 2018, pp. 293–336.

Escola v. Coca Cola Bottling Co., 150 P.2d 436 (Cal. 1944).

Farmer, Charles M., "Relationships of Frontal Offset Crash Test Results to Real-World Driver Fatality Rates," *Traffic Injury Prevention*, Vol. 6, No. 1, 2005, pp. 31–37.

Farmer, Charles M., David S. Zuby, Joann K. Wells, and Laurie A. Hellinga, "Relationship of Dynamic Seat Ratings to Real-World Neck Injury Rates," *Traffic Injury Prevention*, Vol. 9, No. 6, 2008, pp. 561–567.

Geistfeld, Mark A., "A Roadmap for Autonomous Vehicles: State Tort Liability, Automobile Insurance, and Federal Safety Regulation," *California Law Review*, Vol. 105, No. 6, 2017, pp. 1611–1694.

Gusman, Phil, "The Glaring 'Fault' in No Fault," *Insurance Advocate*, Vol. 117, No. 8, April 10, 2006, pp. 21–22.

Halsey, Ashley, III, "Driverless Cars Promise Far Greater Mobility for the Elderly and People with Disabilities," *Washington Post*, November 23, 2017.

Heaney555, "Waymo Explains What 'Remote Operators' Do," *Reddit*, December 9, 2019. As of October 2, 2020:
https://www.reddit.com/r/SelfDrivingCars/comments/e8bfse/waymo_explains_what_remote_operators_do/

Higgins, Tim, "Driverless Cars Still Handled by Humans—from Afar," *Wall Street Journal*, June 5, 2018.

Highway Traffic Act, R.S.O. 1990, c. H.8. As of October 7, 2020:
https://www.ontario.ca/laws/statute/90h08

Holmes, Oliver Wendell, Jr., *The Common Law*, London: Macmillan, 1881.

Howard, L. S., "Markel Subsidiary State National to Provide Fronting for Tesla's New Insurance Venture," *Insurance Journal*, May 2, 2019. As of February 14, 2020:
https://www.insurancejournal.com/news/national/2019/05/02/525317.htm

IBC—*See* Insurance Bureau of Canada.

Insurance Bureau of Canada, *Auto Insurance for Automated Vehicles: Preparing for the Future of Mobility*, 2018. As of October 1, 2020:
http://www.ibc.ca/on/the-future/automated-vehicles

Insurance Information Institute, "No-Fault Insurance Fraud in New York State Is Ramping Up Premiums," undated. As of July 22, 2020:
https://www.iii.org/article/no-fault-insurance-fraud-new-york-state-ramping-premiums

Insurance Research Council, *Third-Party Bad Faith in Florida's Automobile Insurance System*, Malvern, Pa., August 2014.

———, "Study Estimates Florida Third-Party Bad-Faith Costs at $7.6 Billion for 12-Year Period (2006–2017)," press release, Malvern, Pa., September 18, 2018. As of October 4, 2020:
https://www.insurance-research.org/sites/default/files/downloads/NR_IRC_FLbadfaith_SEPT2018.pdf

IRC—*See* Insurance Research Council.

James, Fleming, Jr., "Contribution Among Joint Tortfeasors: A Pragmatic Criticism," *Harvard Law Review*, Vol. 54, No. 7, May 1941, pp. 1156–1169.

Kalra, Nidhi, James M. Anderson, and Martin Wachs, *Liability and Regulation of Autonomous Vehicle Technologies*, Berkeley, Calif.: California Partners for Advanced Transportation Technology Program, University of California Institute of Transportation Studies, UCB-ITS-PRR-2009-28, 2009.

Landes, William M., and Richard A. Posner, *The Economic Structure of Tort Law*, Cambridge, Mass.: Harvard University Press, 1987.

"Lax U.S. Oversight of Industry Jeopardizes Public Safety," *Status Report*, Vol. 53, No. 4, August 7, 2018, pp. 10–11. As of August 4, 2019:
https://itd.idaho.gov/wp-content/autonomous/Status-Report-Reality-Check_IIHS_Aug-18.pdf

Logue, Kyle D., "The Deterrence Case for Comprehensive Automaker Enterprise Liability," *Journal of Law and Mobility*, Vol. 2019, No. 1, 2019, pp. 1–31. As of October 2, 2020:
https://repository.law.umich.edu/cgi/viewcontent.cgi?article=1001&context=jlm

Marchant, Gary E., and Rachel A. Lindor, "The Coming Collision Between Autonomous Vehicles and the Liability System," *Santa Clara Law Review*, Vol. 52, No. 4, 2012, pp. 1321–1340.

Moorcraft, Bethan, "Tesla and Insurance: Everything You Need to Know," *Insurance Business America*, September 6, 2019. As of July 29, 2020:
https://www.insurancebusinessmag.com/us/guides/
tesla-and-insurance--everything-you-need-to-know-177272.aspx

National Academies of Sciences, Engineering, and Medicine, *A Look at the Legal Environment for Driverless Vehicles*, Washington, D.C.: National Academies Press, 2016. As of October 1, 2020:
https://www.nap.edu/catalog/23453/a-look-at-the-legal-environment-for-driverless-vehicles

National Childhood Vaccine Injury Act of 1986, Pub. L. No. 99-660, Title III, 100 Stat. 3756 (1986). As of October 1, 2020:
https://uscode.house.gov/statviewer.htm?volume=100&page=3756

National Highway Traffic Safety Administration, U.S. Department of Transportation, "Automated Vehicles for Safety," undated a. As of February 14, 2020:
https://www.nhtsa.gov/technology-innovation/automated-vehicles-safety

———, "Driver Assistance Technologies," undated b. As of October 2, 2020:
https://www.nhtsa.gov/equipment/driver-assistance-technologies

———, "Critical Reasons for Crashes Investigated in the National Motor Vehicle Crash Causation Survey," *Traffic Safety Facts*, DOT HS 812 115, February 2015. As of February 14, 2020:
https://crashstats.nhtsa.dot.gov/Api/Public/ViewPublication/812115

———, "2015 Motor Vehicle Crashes: Overview," *Traffic Safety Facts*, DOT HS 812 318, August 2016. As of February 14, 2020:
https://crashstats.nhtsa.dot.gov/Api/Public/ViewPublication/812318

———, "USDOT Releases 2016 Fatal Traffic Crash Data," press release, Washington, D.C., NHTSA 01-17, October 6, 2017. As of November 15, 2020:
https://www.nhtsa.gov/press-releases/usdot-releases-2016-fatal-traffic-crash-data

———, "U.S. Transportation Secretary Elaine L. Chao Announces Further Decreases in Roadway Fatalities," press release, October 22, 2019. As of February 14, 2020:
https://www.nhtsa.gov/press-releases/roadway-fatalities-2018-fars

National Safety Council, "Overview," *Injury Facts*, undated. As of February 14, 2020:
https://injuryfacts.nsc.org/motor-vehicle/overview/introduction/

National Transport Commission, *Motor Accident Injury Insurance and Automated Vehicles*, discussion paper, Melbourne, Victoria, October 2018. As of February 14, 2020:
https://www.ntc.gov.au/sites/default/files/assets/files/NTC%20Discussion%20Paper%20-%20
Motor%20Accident%20Injury%20Insurance%20and%20Automated%20Vehicles.pdf

———, *Motor Accident Injury Insurance and Automated Vehicles*, policy paper, Melbourne, Victoria, August 2019. As of February 14, 2020:
https://www.ntc.gov.au/sites/default/files/assets/files/
Motor-accident-injury-insurance-and-automated-vehicles-August-2019.pdf

Neraas, Mary Beth, "The National Childhood Vaccine Injury Act of 1986: A Solution to the Vaccine Liability Crisis?" *Washington Law Review*, Vol. 63, No. 1, 1988, pp. 149–168.

NHTSA—*See* National Highway Traffic Safety Administration.

NTC—*See* National Transport Commission.

Pace, Nicholas M., and Lloyd Dixon, *Assigning Responsibility Following a Catastrophe: Alternatives to Relying Solely on Traditional Civil Litigation*, Santa Monica, Calif.: RAND Corporation, RR-1597-RC, 2017. As of July 20, 2020:
https://www.rand.org/pubs/research_reports/RR1597.html

Pearl, Tracy Hresko, "Compensation at the Crossroads: Autonomous Vehicles and Alternative Victim Compensation Schemes," *William and Mary Law Review*, Vol. 60, No. 5, April 2019, pp. 1827–1891.

Price–Anderson Nuclear Industries Indemnity Act, Pub. L. No. 85-256, 71 Stat. 576 (1957). As of October 4, 2020:
https://www.govinfo.gov/content/pkg/STATUTE-71/pdf/STATUTE-71-Pg576.pdf

Priest, George L., "The Invention of Enterprise Liability: A Critical History of the Intellectual Foundations of Modern Tort Law," *Journal of Legal Studies*, Vol. 14, No. 3, December 1985, pp. 461–527.

Rabin, Robert L., "Some Thoughts on the Efficacy of a Mass Toxics Administration Compensation Scheme," *Maryland Law Review*, Vol. 52, No. 4, 1993, art. 5.

Ridgway, Derry, "No-Fault Vaccine Insurance: Lessons from the National Vaccine Injury Compensation Program," *Journal of Health Politics, Policy and Law*, Vol. 24, No. 1, February 1999, pp. 59–90.

Road Traffic Act, Japanese House of Councillors, as amended May 28, 2019.

Road Transport Vehicle Act, Japanese House of Councillors, as revised May 17, 2019. As of November 15, 2020, in Japanese:
https://elaws.e-gov.go.jp/search/elawsSearch/elaws_search/lsg0500/detail?lawId=326AC0000000185

Robinette, Christopher J., "Types of Coverage," in Jeffrey E. Thomas, ed., *New Appleman on Insurance, Law Library Edition*, Vol. 6: *Motor Vehicle Insurance*, New Providence, N.J.: LexisNexis, 2020, § 61.03.

Shepardson, David, and Paul Lienert, "Exclusive: In Boost to Self-Driving Cars, U.S. Tells Google Computers Can Qualify as Drivers," *Reuters Technology News*, Washington/Detroit, February 9, 2016. As of February 14, 2020:
https://www.reuters.com/article/us-alphabet-autos-selfdriving-exclusive-idUSKCN0VJ00H

Stanley, Karlyn D., and Jason Wagner, *Revolutionizing Our Roadways: Data Privacy Considerations for Automated and Connected Vehicles*, College Station, Tex.: Texas A&M Transportation Institute, November 2015. As of February 14, 2020:
https://static.tti.tamu.edu/tti.tamu.edu/documents/TTI-2015-13.pdf

Statistics Department, National Safety Council, "NSC Motor Vehicle Fatality Estimates," March 27, 2018.

Telematics Task Force, *Telematics Data Definition*, white paper, December 2014. As of November 15, 2020:
http://www.eti-home.org/Telematics/ftp-telematics/Task%20Force/
Telematics-Data-Definition-White-Paper-12-10-copy.pdf

Teoh, Eric R., and Adrian K. Lund, "IIHS Side Crash Test Ratings and Occupant Death Risk in Real-World Crashes," *Traffic Injury Prevention*, Vol. 12, No. 5, 2011, pp. 500–507.

Transport Canada, *Safety Assessment for Automated Driving Systems in Canada*, January 2019. As of November 19, 2020:
https://tc.canada.ca/sites/default/files/migrated/tc_safety_assessment_for_ads_s.pdf

Travelers Institute, *Insuring Autonomy: How Auto Insurance Can Adapt to Changing Risks*, Washington, D.C., July 2018. As of October 1, 2020:
https://www.travelers.com/iw-documents/travelers-institute/
Final-Digital-2018-0710-AV-White-Paper-No-SAE.pdf

T. S., "How Does a Self-Driving Car Work?" *The Economist*, May 12, 2015.

UK Law Commission and Scottish Law Commission—*See* United Kingdom Law Commission and Scottish Law Commission.

UK Public General Acts—*See* United Kingdom Public General Acts.

United Kingdom Law Commission and Scottish Law Commission, *Automated Vehicles: Consultation Paper 2 on Passenger Services and Public Transport*, Law Commission Consultation Paper 245/Scottish Law Commission Discussion Paper 169, London, October 19, 2019. As of October 1, 2020:
https://www.lawcom.gov.uk/project/automated-vehicles/

United Kingdom Public General Acts, 1988 Chapter 52, Road Traffic Act 1988. As of December 2, 2020:
https://www.legislation.gov.uk/ukpga/1988/52/contents

U.S. Census Bureau, *Statistical Abstract of the United States: 2012*, Washington, D.C., August 2011. As of October 1, 2020:
https://www.census.gov/library/publications/2011/compendia/statab/131ed.html

U.S. Code, Title 42, The Public Health and Welfare; Chapter 6A, Public Health Service; Subchapter XIX, Vaccines; Part 2, National Vaccine Injury Compensation Program. As of October 2, 2020:
https://uscode.house.gov/view.xhtml?path=/prelim@title42/chapter6A/subchapter19/
part2&edition=prelim

U.S. Code, Title 42, The Public Health and Welfare; Chapter 23, Development and Control of Atomic Energy; Division A, Atomic Energy; Subchapter XIII, General Authority of Commission; Section 2210, Indemnification and Limitation of Liability. As of October 2, 2020:
https://uscode.house.gov/view.xhtml?req=(title:42%20section:2210%20edition:prelim)%20OR%20
(granuleid:USC-prelim-title42-section2210)&f=treesort&edition=prelim&num=0&jumpTo=true

Weinrib, Ernest J., *The Idea of Private Law*, New York: Oxford University Press, 2012.

Wells, Catharine Pierce, "Tort Law as Corrective Justice: A Pragmatic Justification for Jury Adjudication," *Michigan Law Review*, Vol. 88, No. 8, August 1990, pp. 2348–2413.

Westenberg, Brian, Kristin Kolodge, Tina Georgieva, and Lisa Boor, *Automated Vehicles: Liability Crash Course*, Troy, Mich.: J. D. Power and Miller Canfield, March 2018. As of October 1, 2020:
https://www.millercanfield.com/media/article/
200479_JDP_Miller%20Canfield%20MCity%20White%20Paper_2018_Final.pdf

Winkelman, Zev, Maya Buenaventura, James M. Anderson, Nahom M. Beyene, Pavan Katkar, and Gregory Cyril Baumann, *Hacked Autonomous Vehicles: Who May Be Liable for Damages? An Initial Investigation into How Civil Liability Systems Can Prepare*, Santa Monica, Calif.: RAND Corporation, RB-10063-RC, 2019a. As of October 2, 2020:
https://www.rand.org/pubs/research_briefs/RB10063.html

———, *When Autonomous Vehicles Are Hacked, Who Is Liable?* Santa Monica, Calif.: RAND Corporation, RR-2654-RC, 2019b. As of October 2, 2020:
https://www.rand.org/pubs/research_reports/RR2654.html

Xu, Xian, and Chiang-Ku Fan, "Autonomous Vehicles, Risk Perceptions and Insurance Demand: An Individual Survey in China," *Transportation Research Part A: Policy and Practice*, Vol. 124, June 2019, pp. 549–556.

Zipursky, Benjamin C., "Civil Recourse, Not Corrective Justice," *Georgetown Law Journal*, Vol. 91, 2003, pp. 695–756.

Zuby, David, *Consumer Safety Information Programs at IIHS*, Arlington, Va.: Insurance Institute for Highway Safety, Paper 15-0228, undated. As of November 15, 2020:
https://www-esv.nhtsa.dot.gov/Proceedings/24/files/24ESV-000228.PDF

CPSIA information can be obtained
at www.ICGtesting.com
Printed in the USA
BVHW012305120421
R12106200001B/R121062PG603568BVX00026B/3